BECOMING AN
INVESTOR:

The First 100 Days

Farah C. Jaber

ISBN: 978-1-6847-0786-7 (sc)
ISBN: 978-1-6847-0785-0 (e)

Library of Congress Control Number: 2019911461

Lulu Publishing Services rev. date: 08/07/2019

The Personal Journal of
A Young Investor On His Journey
Towards Financial Freedom

This book is dedicated to:

My Late Father
My Wonderful Mother
My Lovely Wife
My Twin Brother

DAY 1

I started my journey towards Financial Freedom on January 30th 2018, when I had 2,600 USD I could spare, with the intent to change my life forever from that point on. I made multiple moves on that year, as I had no real investing strategy. I listened to the financial news, followed some of their advice, read a few articles and followed their advice as well. I did not do enough research and when the markets went down, I gave in to my emotions and sold stocks at a loss.

I believe the failure of that year allowed me to learn valuable lessons and I decided to review my approach entirely in 2019. Nevertheless, I achieved a tremendous victory in 2018, I had managed to save more than 50% of my salary consistently throughout that year. I was therefore ready to take on 2019. I learned, I perfected my knowledge, I refocused and here I am ready to share my journey to financial success, one day at a time.

As of today, my portfolio value stands at USD 50,816.94 almost a 1,000 USD jump from yesterday mainly due to the trust investors have placed into Apple and Microsoft, driving their stock value up respectively by 3.68% and 2.30%.

Positive or negative fluctuations overnight on the stock market is normal and you must stay focused on the long term, as throughout history, stocks have always performed well and gained value over time.

That brings me back to the purpose of this book. When I decided to change my financial fate last year, it was critical to educate myself and elevate my financial literacy; I understandably looked online first for content that could help me, I went on YouTube, and it looked like everyone was trying to sell me something. I just could not find content that was practical or rich enough to allow me to reflect on my own situation and make real progress.

I went on podcast platforms, I typed the words "investor" and there were series of podcasts but all made for the advanced or seasoned investor by seasoned investors. I needed to know more but none focused on the actual process of getting there. It was therefore paramount to educate myself by consolidating all the contents from all possible platforms on the internet, reading hundreds of articles frequently, reading financial statements, researching technical terms in more details and talking to people. All of this have happened because I decided to take the leap of faith into investing and overcoming that fear of potentially losing everything. It all started from there.

I am certainly not a writer or one of those speakers that pumps you up for your day. I think it was simply important to create a book and a podcast with a genuine objective, not only to share the day to day journey of one trying to reach life changing financial objectives but also to try and assist others who have that same intent.

I will be entirely honest, I am doing this for myself as well in order to stay disciplined and right there on my path. It is a sort of therapy, as anyone knowing me personally can testify that I loved to spend money and never had any plans with it for my future: basically "the perfect customer".

It does not matter how much money you make, what type of work you do or how much your family depends on you, the important thing is to start re-evaluating yourself and find within your source of income a percentage you can allocate to invest. With even 100 dollars per month, you can own company shares that pay dividends.

I believe the most important burden to tackle as of today is to review your lifestyle, clear any outstanding debts and start investing that extra cash.

Easier said than done for sure, but we all know the meaning of working hard and I am sure you can put the same level of efforts you pour out daily at your work place into making sure you start rebalancing your finances to create wealth, starting today. I started investing with 2,600 USD and you will witness through this journey that I will reach my objectives through discipline, hard work and patience.

Allow me to share with you the names of a few people who have helped me at multiple levels and over a short period of time by me just taking the time to listen to them. They would be a good start:

- Gary Vaynerchuk or GaryVee: you can find him on all existing social media platforms and he has a great podcast as well. This guy simply pours unlimited amount of value to his listeners and is simply practical. He will focus on mindset, self-awareness and positivity. A good person to follow and will certainly continue to touch many people's lives.

- Warren Buffett: legendary investor and one of the richest persons in the world. He keeps it simple really and is fascinating to listen to. I keep track of his investments and it certainly does not hurt to align with him in your own investment strategy, because if he decides to purchase stocks of a company, you can be sure he did the homework and sees growth in that company in the upcoming 10 years.

I will document my journey as of now, wherein each journal entry will reflect my thoughts, challenges, failures, victories and concerns. It will allow for a deep immersion into the actual process that will lead me to financial freedom....or not.

DAY 2

Today the value of my portfolio is USD49,932.05 or a general drop of 938.74 USD from yesterday. Remember when I said that large, overnight fluctuations both positive and negative are normal? I did reach a portfolio value of USD 51,000USD yesterday, only to drop back to previous levels of two days ago. Such an occurrence must not trigger you to sell any of your positions, as there are reasons why the stocks lost value yesterday, but that is not important, as you are in it for the long term.

On the contrary, I see a great opportunity here. All of my stocks have lost their value and one of them, Bank of America dropped by 4.15% yesterday and reached a level of 7.97% below what I have paid! I see this as an opportunity to increase my position with Bank of America. Doing this will lower the average price you paid for the company, hence giving you more opportunity for growth.

However, do you know my weakness here? I did not keep cash aside that would allow me to take advantage of these sorts of opportunities and I will certainly not sell any other stock in my portfolio to do this. It is food for thought to always keep cash on hand. It will be up to me to determine the proportion of my savings kept aside in the event of a large negative stock market fluctuation, so I have the buying power to purchase discounted stocks of the companies in my portfolio or the ones you are keeping an eye on. All I hope for now is that this stock will remain at this level for another 8 or 9 days, until I receive my salary.

Now, after this major failure of mine, let's talk about the tools that support me in my journey towards financial freedom. Please note that I receive no compensation from them, this is your step by step toolbox:

1. Pocket Expense Pro

This will allow you to budget and keep track of your expenses. It will show you, once you have populated the app with your data, exactly where you stand in terms of the evolution of your net worth, cash flow position, your income and your expenses.

More importantly, once you have done that exercise for the whole year like me, it will give you your objective at year end.

2. Saxo Capital Markets

This is my brokerage firm on which I am performing all my operations. It is based out of Singapore, has a solid reputation (you can research this online and ask around) and they have a user-friendly investing platform, allowing you to invest in stocks, bonds, commodities etc.... however, I only look at stocks. Being user-friendly is very important to the new investor and it gives you news and insights from their team of experts if ever they are relevant to you. Their commission base is 3.99 USD per transaction, which is very reasonable. They are Highly recommended but they do not operate in the United States yet.

3. Yahoo Finance

Great source of news and information and they also have very detailed data on each listed companies. Once you have taken the previous steps of making your budget, and opening your brokerage account, it will be time to enter your holdings into that app to track your stock and portfolio performance. The app will also give you real time stock movement when markets are open with a delay. We are not traders, we are long term investors, so we do not mind the daily fluctuations. It works for us just fine.

4. Seeking Alpha

I really love this app; it is a great source of information as it is a platform which not only contains daily articles written by experts but also by regular investors like you or me, who are sharing their analysis of the market and of your stocks. Once you enter your holdings in the app, it will feed you targeted news and articles on the companies you have invested in. It allows you as well to form your own opinions, as the information you receive is usually unbiased.

5. News 360 and Google News

I highly recommend you download these apps as you can customize your newsfeed to send you only information you are interested in. Apart from your hobbies, you can customize it to feed you mainstream information on the companies' CEO, product and analysis of all kinds targeted onto the companies you have invested in. This will allow you to form your own opinion and stay informed about companies and industries you are aiming at investing into.

DAY 3

Today is Sunday and all markets are closed, however, I do look forward to the Apple event tomorrow! This could be the start of a new era for Apple and we will learn more on Monday.

On Sundays, I remember I used to go to a few malls around the city of Bangkok, when I lived there and release some of that weekly stress accumulated at work into some shopping. I was convinced it was very well deserved after all and that's what I kept saying to myself before triggering a buy and again spend money, rather than invest. I remember going full on around the shops for clothes, electronics, home décor, high end groceries and finish the day by hop into an Uber, but not any Uber...the Uber Black; twice the price! I remember then asking my wife, "How much do you think we spent today?" We used to guess and it ended up being 600 or 700USD of items (which I do not even remember) and that would be every single weekend, not accounting for restaurants or other things. Doing the math, that was 3500 USD per month on THINGS. I would have tripled my net worth today if I simply had a different mindset.

I climbed the corporate ladder, worked hard and with passion to reach a high level in my organization; it was all I knew. Work, play, save nothing and thinking that somehow, I had no need to plan a future or provide myself with life options. But I still wanted to make it to the top, which I suppose was a delusion. To have a choice in life is what we should all be aiming for I believe and it does start by having liquidity and a lot of it. It took a while for me to jump start my brain into the right mindset.

So when did I realize that I was an idiot? I posted on my Instagram page pictures of a trip that I had made with close friends, where we rented a yacht, out of all things, for a few days. Full service, as well because we wanted a taste of what we could not afford. I came back home with a few pictures and a few laughs, but I had no joy, as happiness does not lie in such things, regardless of the price tags. While scrolling through Netflix one day, I stumbled onto a documentary called Minimalism, which was a splendid view of the world and it addressed my mental issues quickly. I am not a Minimalist but I kept very valuable principles until today, which triggered a self-improvement, self-education spree and taking me a month to discover a new passion about what I actually hated the most from school days until my day to day at 38 years old: Corporate Finance and The Stock Market. I was always afraid of deep diving into them, afraid to not be smart enough to understand, that it was for the smarter guys and not a regular person like me. I was dead wrong. We are smarter than we think, and we have access to the greatest source of knowledge ever: The Internet. It is opening up unlimited options for me and I make sure to grasp everything I could that would teach me how to invest. There is no need for online courses that costs thousands of dollars, when you can do this all by yourself

I started the journey that will see my net worth today increase by 20 times since January 2018. For all the big spenders out there, the consumers, I have good news for you- it feels even better to invest your cash than to spend on dumb items to impress people you hate and that bring no value whatsoever to your life. Every month, when I pay myself, I feel like I have achieved all my goals for the month, I am pumped and ready to go back to work to increase my income (meaning being promoted or get that yearly bonus). It triggers a chain of events that you did not expect to be possible. I am now working on two other sources of income, even though they are flat now, you will witness them grow. After that growth, hopefully we will be talking about your own journey when the book and podcast mature.

That is the mindset of the new investor, an unlimited source of energy towards achieving financial goals. I have left my old life behind forever, so it is all upside from now on. Jere is what I learned:

1. Stop spending immediately on things that do not bring value to your life;

2. Assess your current financial situation

3. Start clearing your outstanding debt;

4. Open a brokerage account, even if you have pennies to invest in the beginning;

5. Once debt is cleared, all your extra cash after expenses goes in there;

6. Invest in companies and sector you understand and even love and that produce dividends;

7. Stay informed on the companies you are interested in;

8. Stay disciplined and repeat the process over and over; and

9. Ensure you have a yearly objective and go for it.

DAY 4

It is Monday morning today in Asia where I live and the region's stock markets have opened but New York is still sleeping. Asia's markets have nevertheless opened on the negative, which is usually an indicator of today's New York Stock Exchange performance at open. In my long-term intent to build other sources of income, my yearly dividends now stand at 753.73USD with the current positions on my portfolio.

I was approached online recently about the reasons why I divulge my holdings, and that most probably it was not real money, as no one in his right mind would share such information. I always appreciate feedback as I am a hotelier by heart, but I believe that transparency is key in documenting my own journey towards financial freedom. I have a firm belief that by doing so, I will help others in taking their own leap of faith and start building their wealth, showing that it is in fact not rocket science.

Thank you for your valuable feedback but I will keep posting my portfolio performance daily to let everyone know of my every move and support those moves by illustrating them.

Today is a good day to talk about income and if you already have a steady source or sources of income, how important it is to continuously strive to grow it by not allowing your expenses to grow proportionally to your income growth and keep ensuring you build wealth.

First and foremost, make sure your highest source of income has a strong potential to grow. What I mean by that is, excel in your current profession and be an expert at your craft. If you are not happy in your current job, then there is no way you can grow your income from it, as you do not have the drive or passion to excel. My feelings on this is to move on from it immediately, get a job you love that may pay you less, excel at it and grow your income through promotions/bonus or salary increases but most important in all this is to LOVE WHAT YOU DO. Believe me when I say this, I wake up every Monday looking forward to my week, passion is strong and therefore it does not feel like work. Then amazing things happen:

1. I have received yearly bonuses for the past 2 years

2. I have been promoted 4 times since 2016

3. I have doubled my salary in 5 years

Alternatively, of course you can be an ENTREPRENEUR. You may have a great idea/product, so get the funding for it, build that APP and reach that pinnacle of success and become a millionaire in 5 years. Allow me to put things into perspective. There are possibly 1% of entrepreneurs who become successful ones and another 1% that make it through an unbelievable amount of hard work, passion, failures or close to bankruptcy on multiple occasions, then they eventually get there. You hear about them and your first thought is, "THEY ARE LUCKY". No they aren't, as there is no hack or shortcut in this and it is unbelievably hard since you may lose everything three times over. If you feel you are ready for this, go for it and the market will decide to elevate you with the 1%; the odds are high though.

I will try therefore to stay practical here, as most of the readers have a regular job, so ensure you love your job/industry and keep growing your income from it. Once you are in that income growth situation, and you have already taken that step to start investing, the next source of income is one that will take time to build but can turn out to be called a "passive income" resource. If you follow a Dividend Growth strategy with your investment portfolio, basically meaning that each and every investment that you make should go into stocks that produce dividends and that have shown a history of dividend growth, with time, discipline and patience you will be able to produce sufficient dividends to cover a proportion or even all of your expenses. A good way to get to the objective as well is to collect dividends for a full year or quarterly and reinvest them into buying more stocks to create a compounding effect on your portfolio. A dividend growth strategy can also act as a cushion in case there is negativity in the market and your stocks lose value.

There is another way to secure a solid income and low expenses, but most of the people may not be willing to take such life changing measures. Expatriation is a very solid way to gain ground and time towards building wealth. In my case, I have never taken advantage of this unfortunately and as I mentioned before, I changed my mindset only but recently. However, if you have skills, still young and free, moving to another country would seriously have a tremendous impact on your financial situation.

However, you need to be ready to sacrifice a large part of your comfort and life habits. Generally, cost of living is the lowest and salaries the highest in difficult destinations, but such a lifestyle is extremely rewarding at many other levels. Take it from someone who lived and worked in 12 countries from Africa to the Seychelles or Maldives or South East Asia and currently based out from a third tier city in a developing country in Asia. Not easy but allowing to some extent to gain time towards financial freedom.

Are you ready to consider this? What is your actual will to make it? Remember there are no hacks or shortcuts.

DAY 5

March 26th, 2019
Net Worth: 49,512.68 USD

My portfolio value stands at 49,512.68 USD with a yearly dividend income of 753.73 USD. Portfolio value since last Friday has dropped by 485.52USD, on top of another drop in value on Friday last week of 938.74 USD. A total of 1,424.26 USD. Why is this important for me to highlight? Because I would like to show that you should not be emotional about this and you should stay your course because you know for a fact that you have initially made the right choices in your positions.

I am an investor in Apple and got some really exciting news through that Apple event. The new services such as Apple TV+, Apple News+, Apple Arcade and the Apple Credit Card which launched on Monday, have a solid promise for growth and Apple has instantly become a major player in those markets. In my opinion, I foresee serious growth in the long term.

Now back to my portfolio. There are two things that emerge and one of them is that I still have Bank of America as a buy opportunity if the current stock price sticks until the end of the month, so I receive my salary and potentially will consider increasing my position. However, there is a more important issue here which remains: I do not have any cash on hand. I only have 268 USD built through dividend payments this year and cash residues.

This is certainly not sufficient at all. I need to tackle that weakness in my portfolio and fix this moving forward; my aim is to always have enough cash on hand to take those potentially once in a lifetime opportunities when the markets start to melt. A quasi-certainty but we simply cannot predict when.

The US economy and its stock market have been very healthy for the past decade and it is only a matter of time before you will be able to purchase great companies at a discounted stock price. I will let you know however later how I can still have that sitting cash work for me, while we patiently wait for that market meltdown.

Where will I get that cash? I mentioned how important it is for you to be genuinely happy at your present which will allow you to continuously grow your income through promotions, salary increases and bonuses.

As a happy worker, I managed to hit my targets last year which unlocked a yearly bonus; a humble hotelier bonus I assure you. Most people would use this extra cash to buy more things or go on that vacation. I did that before. However, I will reinvest 90% of it in my brokerage account and next month, you will see my cash position seriously increase as I have also committed to keep it on hand through the month of April. I will keep on building this cash position monthly as well, most probably allocating 20% of my investment money in it and the rest into my current companies or a newcomer I would have studied.

I would like to emphasize once again that the aim of this book is to document my own journey towards financial freedom. A simple illustration for the young and new investor on the steps I am taking towards this goal so it could potentially inspire him or her to take that leap of faith and start their own journey today. The underlying principle remains the same: Start spending much less than you make and reinvest your money, change your lifestyle, your habits and start paying yourself first. There are plenty of information online, but I have chosen to document this daily until I reach my own goal.

DAY 6

March 27th 2019
Net Worth: 49,301.59 USD

My portfolio at market close is down again by 0.37% with a surprising decline of the Apple stock, my largest holding, by 1.03%. If you are like me, lucky to live in a different time zone, take full advantage of it as the New York Stock Exchange opens at dinner time and closes when you are fast asleep, so I have very little chances to be tempted into day trading. The same attitude should be adopted if I was lucky enough to live in the United States as well, to let the Stock Market do its work for me whether I am up or down. I am in it for the long term. If you perform some research on the history of the stock market since inception until today, you would understand my point very clearly, your portfolio will look sensational in 10 or 15 years if only you stay disciplined and stick by your investment choices. Do not sell your positions until you retire. Do not sell your positions until you have reached your financial goals.

I wanted to spend some time on the Financial Goals. I spoke yesterday to two young managers in my hotels and I asked each of them what their definition of financial success was. They are respectively 27 and 38 years old, one is female we will name Mary and the other male we will name John. One is from Europe and the other is local. Mary said that she would consider herself financially successful if she attained a net worth of 5 Million USD in 10 years. John said that he would be happy with a guaranteed lifetime 2000 USD/month, which represents over 50 years, a total net worth of 1,200,000

USD, he said he does not require more than this to live comfortably in this Asian country. Let's assume it takes him 10 years to accomplish this and reach his targeted net worth, he will need to be able to save 120,000 USD per year or 10,000 USD per month. A difficult task, meaning that he would need to climb that corporate ladder first which should take him 15 years and start saving then for another 10 years every month without fail.

There are many milestones to reach here, but that is not impossible as in 25 years he will still be young and he would have attained his objective through hard work, dedication, passion and drive. That would be the classic route to take evidently and nobody has so much patience, however I am a very firm believer that the times we live in have tremendously changed and if you have a dream you can attain it much faster thanks to the internet, you can monetize your passions or hobbies now online.

There are no more excuses possible as to why you cannot achieve your dreams, the internet exposed your weaknesses as an achiever, you only need to act, and the market will decide if you are good enough, no longer another human being. Both Mary and John have a shot at their dreams now regardless of their targeted net worth, a thing that was simply impossible only a 15 years ago.

Mary's objective seems however quite a stretch unless you have created a disruptor on the market, unless you have found a problem and fixed it through your innovation or you have become one of those influencers online and you touched everyone's hearts in a way or another, possible but the odds of that are evidently high. She could consistently beat the stock market over a few years, received a call from a scout from a large investment fund, got the job, excelled at the tasks and consistently received a seven figure bonus, possible but another hard path.

My point here overall is there are no shortcuts, there are no hacks in building wealth or achieving your dreams. All the paths are hard, but they can be walked, it will be about YOU, no one else will do it for you or set you up.

I will need, to rewire myself throughout this journey, adopt the mindset of an achiever, make the right sacrifices, and increase my income through drive and passion at my current job and side ventures. It will all rest upon my ability to save and invest consistently with discipline and patience. We live only once and I am young, therefore my greatest asset is TIME, but

I am also older, therefore my other greatest asset is EXPERIENCE, and both have the ability to be monetized. It is not too early or too late to start the journey towards my financial freedom. Some may say that I should not always think about money, I will agree, but money here is only the end goal, what will make me happy is the process in between as it will fulfill me to levels beyond my current understanding, I will discover new skills that were probably sleeping within me, I will taste the sweetness of victories and the bitterness of defeats but I will prevail at the end as I have already set myself up for success by taking these first steps into saving and investing.

DAY 9

March 29th, 2019
Net Worth: 49,958.61 USD

Today at market close my portfolio has finally picked up a little. It is up by 0.24% and while it does not make up the week, it is always good to see progress however small it may be or however slow you feel it is. As mentioned earlier, I do have a yearly financial objective which I will achieve regardless of the obstacles along the way, the temptations or people telling you things like "you live only once..." or "you will not take that money to your grave" or "I want to live today not tomorrow..."

Let's just say that the Universe will throw at me all sorts of reasons or events that will get in my way to achieving my objectives or to give up along the way. It will require me to take action as to change my story but I will also need to be attentive. The Universe brings more positivity into your life than you can imagine, giving you all the reasons to actually succeed in pretty much anything you decide to venture into. Money here is just the objective, a motivator, a tool to give you a little bit more freedom and security but ultimately we are talking about the pursuit of happiness. Happiness I believe is in the process of getting to your objective not in the end game.

I have had a tremendous amount of fun just starting this book and the podcast. For example, the Universe is not giving me subscribers as of yet, it is telling me to stop and do something else that way but it is also telling me to continue and to do a podcast episode practically daily, the process of doing this project is where happiness lies. The Universe is also challenging every single components of success; your patience, your perseverance, your level of self-awareness. I AM the Universe and the beauty of it is that I can control the outcome.

How can I control the Universe and ultimately myself? The actual control fuel lies in surrounding myself with positivity. I wanted to spend some time on this as I feel this is key to the whole mechanism towards success. I will surround myself with positive people, with achievers, with people who have the same level of energy and aspirations. Don't get me wrong, I am not talking about hanging with people with money or in a specific social class I aspire to be part of. I can admire them if they bring value into my life but I am not them. I will succeed on my own terms, my story is different than anybody else's, I will stay focused and not get distracted by things that will not contribute to my own progress. I will ensure that the time I allocate to any of my activities is getting me closer to my goal. I will stay laser focused. It is imperative that I cut out negative people or negative thoughts from my life. This is hard at times as we are emotional beings. However, should it get hard, I will then feed myself with positivity and there is plenty of content out there to rebalance my thoughts, until the day I am trained enough to that respect to prevent negativity from even getting close to me. My main source of positivity for example lies in classical music which for me is pure food to my soul. We always have a mean of escape in whatever form.

I also love calling my Mom as she has already reached that pinnacle of positivity. She has beaten every single challenge put in her way because of her positivity and her almost divine understanding of this principle. Listening to her resets all my meters back to Positive. Find your sources of positivity and ensure you are hooked on them on your journey towards the accomplishment of your objectives, in this case your financial freedom.

The young investor must look at his actions and habits in detail; understand the negative impact instant gratification can have on his long-term goals. As an example, in the United States I understand that a Starbucks coffee can cost you up to $5, a full options coffee probably. Let's say you need this every morning (for some reason you are unable to pour yourself a two cents cup at home, oversleeping? laziness?). It will cost you $150/month or $1'800 per year. I am a hotelier and I guarantee you that with this kind of money, you can stay in my 5-star resort in paradise for a full week!

Saving that $5 coffee will save you an entire vacation if that is what you are planning this year (remember, even vacation can be rescheduled to when you have attained a few financial milestones). It is indeed in the little things, maybe you should save that money and see how gratifying it is, how you will start adding up little ounces of happiness, one drop after the other by simply reviewing your life habits in detail and by keeping a positive approach to all of this. Find the balance but don't punish yourself. That is one example out of many that can be reviewed. By the way, investing these $150 saved that month can actually buy you 5 shares of Bank of America and pay you dividends of 27 cents per month, hence covering your home freshly brewed coffee expense for your lifetime. What do you think about that!?

DAY 10

My inspiration for today's journal entry came from my wife. She asked me today if I had completed my Podcast episode and I told her that I had not. I did not stay true to my word to make one episode every day or two. This has led me to talk about the value of DISCIPLINE.

So, to get back to the main purpose, something quite interesting happened this week on top of what happened this evening which again taught me that valuable lesson on the value of discipline. I will not waste any time learning valuable lessons then fail to take action afterwards.

There have been multiple fluctuations this week on my portfolio performance which ended up at market close on Friday at 49,958.61 USD or a jump of 0.99% elevating my year to date gains at 17.16%. The interesting point here is that at the same time last week, my portfolio closed at 49'932.05 USD or a 1.86% drop from the previous day. Regardless, the week recovered, and I ended up gaining another 25 USD, the important point here is that I maintained an impeccable discipline level by not selling off my position through that week which ended up on the positive.

Through reading my daily news and articles, another interesting news came up that the S&P 500 (I invite you to research this index please) has seen the best upside since 1998 by almost 13% this quarter this year, what does that tell us? Have you been documenting yourself or have you been able to form your own opinion on your strategy moving forward? Back to my own point of view. Following such upside, prior to 1998, the market has seen in its following ten years, two major crises. As far as I am concerned, I will start building up cash as of Monday 1st of April as promised, as I will receive my regular salary but also a well-deserved bonus for last year.

My short term goals are not ambitious and unattainable. My dream right now, my DREAM is to reach my first milestone or portfolio value of 50,000 USD and remain there. If you have been attentive earlier, when do you think I would be reaching it?

With my bonus injection, I will reach that milestone, next week. There are again no secret to building wealth.

The second milestone is to reach a 75,000 USD portfolio value, and if you allow me I would like to take that challenge while you take your own and take that first step towards financial freedom TODAY.

DAY 11

Today is Sunday, markets are asleep, but I have a great feeling about the week ahead. I am also excited as this week will be the week I will exceed my first 50,000 USD portfolio value milestone.

We need to celebrate small victories as they arise and I am already looking at my next objective, the 75,000 USD milestone which is now on my radar. How about this week will it be the week that you will take your first steps and invest your first dollars? How about this be the week you decide to review your whole approach to your finances and lifestyle? I think it will be the perfect week for anything you may have on your mind right now.

As I previously announced, I will not buy a company or increase my positions this month, I am only injecting the majority of my 2018 bonus in my brokerage account. However, do not let cash sit there, so I will need to find a cash instrument quickly, in which I can still have that cash work for me until buying opportunities arise on the market. Patience is key in this game, and do not feel that you need to buy companies every single month or start drifting towards over-diversification of your portfolio, better stay focused and patient for the right opportunities.

It is important to stay humble on your journey towards financial freedom. Nobody expects a young investor to have it all figured out and asking other people's opinion on your own investment or asking more about theirs will only allow you to keep learning. I will always keep learning on better ways to get my investments to perform. Even my humble podcast is still a source of information for you even if you take 1% of it home. The young investor must continuously document himself, read and research on and about companies as to keep an understanding of the overall dynamics, and build his own opinion. I will not over diversify my portfolio and will rather keep it focused on companies I know, love, follow and value. I will stay committed to my monthly investments, adapt my lifestyle to free investment money, deploy patience while understanding that the journey is a long one, understanding right away that the journey is taken on my own.

I would like to spend some time on the value of Patience. The immediate gratification in today's digital world does not give way to this key principle of financial success as we have a tendency to believe that results will happen overnight or that successful people reached their level of success overnight. We are in a rush to get there rapidly usually to impress people you most probably hate. The science behind success whether it is financial, or any other form, lies in your ability to be patient and persevere through hardship or moments when you feel down or vulnerable. Patience is the virtue of life as we say, as it is a high moral standard and one's ability to endure and persevere.

There was a very interesting thought by Gary Vaynerchuk who said roughly that, "if you are able to listen to a podcast, you are already part of the top 15% on this planet and should basically stop dwelling," and that is very true. For my part, I broadcast my podcast from a third tier city in a developing country in Asia. If you are listening from New York or any other place in the United States of America for example, I think you must take advantage of that privileged situation to work hard towards your dream. In our case the ability to open new sources of income through a new venture, you have all the tools at your disposal and stakeholders to support you, we call that location arbitrage. If I could start something from the dirt here, you can certainly start anything from where you are standing right now.

DAY 13

Through perseverance, discipline, hard work and patience I have been able to reach my first milestone of 50,000 USD. In addition, through passion and resilience, I have been able to grow my income in 2018 through the achievement of my KPI targets for my company, therefore unlocking a bonus. I have as promised injected 90% of my bonus into my brokerage account now reflected in my net worth. My portfolio value at market close reached 59,496.79USD, now getting me closer to the second millstone of 75,000USD. As also promised, I will keep this cash on hand to be ready in the event of a market crash, you will want to have that cash when the companies you want to take position in are on a discount.

Very early on I decided to expatriate myself. Basically since I was 19 years old, I was working and living in different countries than my own. Hospitality business is hard. It is long hours, it is intense, and it is working while others are not. So far I have lived and worked in 12 countries. I was indeed fortunate enough to have been born in a family which could afford my education and did not take on debt. However, I was quickly independent from my parents in terms of sustaining myself financially after my graduation. I worked my way up through the ranks, in difficult environments, in difficult corners of the globe. Believe me, you do not work in Hospitality for the money. We probably have one of the lowest salary scale versus input. I started to really make money when still as an expatriate I had reached higher levels in my organization, today I am General Manager for two luxury hotels. Hard work and Sacrifice have both combined to give a high return on investment over time. Obviously it took me more than 15 years to get there, as I am now 38 years old.

How likely are you to Sacrifice in order to reach your dreams? You need to believe that if I am able today to save so much, have no debt and invest 70% of my income into my future freedom and security (even if I could have done this many years ago, but simple result of my own ignorance), it is because I was very early on willing to Sacrifice a very square way of life in a major city with all its riches. I was willing to do what others may not consider or find too hard, even if I should have started my investment journey earlier. I have made a promise to myself to make up for the time that I have lost which also come with further sacrifice!

As we are today the 2nd of April, I would like to share with you the very first personal finance operations I perform the first day of every month when I receive my income.

1. I pay myself first, so I have transferred my budgeted investment money in my brokerage account.

2. 7% was deducted from my salary for my companies' Joint Investment Program.

3. I pay no income taxes, as they are covered by the company as an expatriate (think about it).

4. I withdrew 900 USD in cash to cover my monthly expenses (groceries and other monthly needs).

5. I settle my American Express for the month of March expenses due to a recent business trip in which I incurred personal expenses as well.

After performing all of this, I can assure you that you are not left with much to spend. You basically live like you are broke which you quickly get used to, but the level of satisfaction and the happiness for a job well done you actually feel are priceless. Go ahead, just try it.

If you are unable to sacrifice too much and I absolutely respect that as only you can determine what you are ready for or what you are not ready for. In that case, the principles and the steps I just mentioned remain the same, spend less than you earn and pay yourself first. Another key aspect is to set milestones for yourself and a yearly financial objective no matter how small or large.

I previously mentioned to review your lifestyle habits. You will need to absolutely ensure that your fixed expenses are kept to a minimum catering for your needs not your wants. This is again another form of Sacrifice with a ridiculous ROI should you take a second look at all this TODAY.

DAY 14

The week has started off on a good foot with further gains on my portfolio elevating its value by 1.10% to USD 59,874.26 mainly driven by Apple, being my highest investment (70%), which took another 1.45% in value, and the Bank of America stock which recovered more than 6% from its dip of last week. I remember when I had no cash on hand to purchase more of it and complained about it to you only last week. However the opportunity may not have been great enough to prompt me to sell any of my other stocks to buy more of that stock. So I increased my position in Bank of America.

If I had some cash on hand I would have definitely bought more to decrease my overall average (this means that by increasing your position on a stock, should you happen to buy it cheaper than the price you originally purchased it for, the overall average price of your lot will therefore decrease giving further room to increase in value). I am on my way to fix that flaw in my strategy already and I promised myself to be cash ready in the future to avoid being a sitting duck and missing opportunities.

Again, your investment strategy or moves should never be driven by emotions but rather by maintaining a good discipline and by doing your homework. Do not approach the stock market or your investment as gambling as it will be the quickest way to lose. Do not approach this to make a quick buck. If this is your aim, please do not go any further. Do not take that journey as it will lead you to utmost dismay and probably total failure.

I am prepared to lose ALL my yearly gains in a single day and it will not affect my emotions. For sure my profile has a higher tolerance to risk but the principle is the same. If you are mentally prepared for the possibility to lose those gains in a single day and take the opportunity that such an event brings, then you are ready to be an investor. Like a hawk flying high above focusing on its prey while awaiting the right moment to strike, then strike when its prey is at its most vulnerable position, be the same with your stocks. Wait for them to be at their most discounted state and go out there with the cash you would have built as of today and strike.

The question everyone asks: How will I know when the stock price of a company is undervalued or overvalued or when it is actually a good time to buy?

This is where the homework you would have done will kick in. Please do rest assured that the greatest investors of all times have tremendous amount of resources both financial and in human capital to do that type of research for them. You will not do a better job on your own across multiple companies, across multiple industries or sectors unless you have an ability that most human beings do not have but I believe I am writing for the majority of us normal people.

My portfolio is composed of only four (4) companies in sectors I am highly interested in or have a hobby knowing more about or their trends or what makes them successful or what would make them successful in the future. Start by reading their 10K (the 10K is the company's annual report that gives you a comprehensive summary of a company's financial performance), that will be a good first step to take. There will be multiple terms in there that you will not understand immediately, BE CURIOUS, research them and try and apply them to your overall understanding of that report. Read the full report, it may be a long read but it is your first step to financial literacy so take it seriously.

There are enough resources online that are free, teaching you all you need to know.

I suggest you also listen to the company's quarterly earnings call to educate yourself further. The quarterly earnings call is a conference call between the management of a public company, analysts, investors and the media to discuss the company's financial results during a given reporting period. That was a clear definition, right? Well it was as simple as typing it in

Google, so no excuses to educate yourselves as it is that easy in 2019. When I was 20, I had to dig into books at the library for weeks to get information, take advantage of your world right now!

The quarterly earnings call can be accessed via the company's website under the Investor Relations section.

How about you pick a listed company today to study, research, and get to know for a full week? How about you allocate 2 hours a day to that exercise?

DAY 16

It was a regular day on the stock market with regards to my stock's portfolio. It lost in value about 75 USD as the company I work stock price lost 2.53% while others did quite well. Getting very close to that 60,000USD threshold though. I am currently looking at Banks stocks, they may be much better stocks out there but one thing is certain in my opinion they will continue to do well in the long term and still pay very good dividends, there will be little chance that you lose it all there.

I will however keep my cash this month and look at another investment probably next month, should I find prices to be fair enough.

There is a crucial aspect I wanted to spend some time on while on that journey to financial freedom, Tony Robbins said something very true along the lines of, *You cannot earn your way to financial freedom, you will need to create other sources of income for yourself.* Once you have started with your first investments, you will therefore need to engage in new ventures on the side that will place you outside your comfort zone or maybe start something you never thought you would be doing. As an example, I am certainly not a professional podcaster or producer, yet I decided to share my journey in this way for the moment. I have no expectations on what this new venture could bring but I take it as a first step into a world of opportunities, and I know for a fact that even if it will not take off, I will not regret doing it... so it is in fact a win/win! Once it matures, who knows, it could become interesting enough to generate some income in the long term.

Along your way you will receive multiple feedback on your new venture, usually negative or average, usually aimed at giving you a reality check from the get-go, discouraging you to continue. However, you must believe in your own capabilities, ensure that your product/service/show/t-shirt or whatever you have decide to venture into, keeps evolving, being watered and cherished... get better at it, learn the craft. I am a firm believer that every human being has tremendous potential, you just need to try things especially if you are in your 20's as you are blessed with an unbelievable amount of time in front of you! The older you get, the more targeted your choice of venture should be given you have slightly less of that time leverage at your disposal.

Do not listen to outside voices along your journey and there will be many of them telling you to stop. If you fail it will not be because someone told you so, it will be because you have not been good enough or that the market has simply not adopted your you or your product. If you fail once, start over again. Patience, Perseverance, Passion, Dedication and Hard Work are the only truths behind success and they all emanate from you. I was told yesterday that my podcast was very average, well it is undoubtedly my fault, and I will have to make it better if I have any hope of it bringing serious value to young investors. It's that simple, be accountable.

The main takeaway here is that whether it is in building wealth from scratch or getting into a new venture, it is a lot of fun trying to get rich! I believe once we have reached a consequent financial goal, doubling it may not make you happy but the journey to get there is already very exciting.

DAY 19

April 8ᵗʰ, 2019
Net Worth: 59,733.58 USD

I hope you are like me looking forward to that week! It also appears that the right thing to do right now is to ensure you have sufficient cash on hand in your brokerage account and while at the risk repeating myself, this is crucial as you need to prepare yourself for the high probability for an upcoming recession in the US Economy and in your lifetime, you may encounter only a few of those.

Now why would I be so positive, indeed as Recessions are good for the investor, for the simple reason that the stock market is heavily discounted, and you can simply shop around for wonderful companies at a great price. Don't get me wrong, no one likes recessions but how else do you think rich people get richer? I will leave you to develop your own theory on this.

I often think how ignorant I was only a couple of years ago, it does help to remember how easy it was for me to spend money on things I did not need. How easy it was for me to accept the fact that I did not have much aside at the end of the month, I did not understand the value of money until I started investing. Since My first investment in January 2018 my net worth rose 2203%

So I am not selling you anything, I am not receiving any compensation for what I am telling you today, I am sharing with you in the simplest of forms how I WILL reach my financial objectives by documenting my day to day, and this will take years. The most successful people on the planet did not document their journey on how they got there, whereas this would have been GOLD to all of us young investors. I am certainly not in that league, but I am posting pretty solid figures already just be following the reasoning I am trying to share with you, documenting failure is as valuable as documenting success.

What would be the steps to take in order to first and foremost get rid of any debt, this will require discipline and you need to start today:

1. Set a Budget

You need to forecast your spending against your income, so you know exactly where you stand. I do mine for the full year and I am very pessimistic when I forecast. I keep all spending to a minimum.

2. Avoid taking on any new debt

Stop borrowing money to consume, it is simply the worst thing you can do. If you must borrow money, do it to invest in a business that would make money.

3. Educate yourself on investing and corporate finance

Do not be afraid, it is simpler than you think, and you do not need to be a captain of the industry to start investing

4. Your subscriptions

What are they? Start re-evaluating your monthly subscriptions. Are they necessary, how often do you use the service? Are they bringing any value to your life? Are they getting you closer to your goal? If not, cancel them all.

5. Increase your income

We have covered this point

6. Use Cash rather than credit cards

I withdraw 900 USD cash every month to pay for my expenses. No credit cards, you will see how easy it becomes to manage your expenses this way.

7. Start selling things you do not need

Do an inventory of your home and declutter. When you see an item, think about when the last time was you used it, does it bring real value to your life, when was the last time you thought of using it. If you can't answer those questions, get rid of it…sell the thing.

This is all at least a good start to get rid of habits aimed at building debt. Paying off your outstanding debt is a priority and there is no excuse for not building additional sources of income to that effect given the world we live in, a world where you can basically start any business from your bedroom. Pay off debt first by growing your income at work, excel in what you do, ensure you are happy in your current job to do so, if not QUIT. Even if in debt, allocate 5% or even 3% to your investments, even if it is small amounts, they will compound over time. Once you have fixed all of this, start increasing your investment money and start thinking in terms of growing your net worth rather than savings.

DAY 20

April 9th 2019
Net Worth: 60,373.54 USD

It was another good day on the stock market as my portfolio increased its value by +1.06% or 546 USD to 60,373.54USD. I have reached that 60,000 USD threshold forecasted last week. It is worth saying that my yearly gains so far have exceeded 20% or close to 9000 USD.

I have no illusions that a net worth fluctuates, and I can easily lose these gains in a few days but let us break this down a little so that should any of the following occurs. There will never be any reason to panic if you have both cash on hand and time:

Should my portfolio lose 10% in its value, they call it a market correction, which in this case would still not make my stocks cheap enough to buy more of, in my point of view, or spark me to sell them off as well for that matter, apart probably from the Bank of America stock that would start becoming interesting when the next correction occurs.

Should my portfolio at this stage lose 20% in its value, we can start calling that a bear market at which point I believe through my own research that all my stocks will deserve re-investing into and it is not yet worth panicking into selling off as well. That is of course my point of view solely based on my own research, tolerance to risk, the patience I am willing to allocate to the recovery period of the stock market which always rebounds stronger over time, and on the fair price I would be ready to pay for my stocks. So again be ready with serious cash on hand when that occurs.

We talk a lot about a possible recession these days in the US economy, which generally occurs when there are two consecutive quarters or more of negative growth in Gross Domestic Product (which is the total value of all goods and services produced in the country). Should a recession occur, it could potentially spark a financial crisis as well which is a much more serious situation indicating a very strong decline of stock prices often caused by panic due to factors in the economy or sparked by other factors I would not be in a position to explain.

What I can be certain of, is that the biggest investors on the planet find period of crisis as a serious opportunity and you should be able to do so as well. We are in it for the long term; we are young, we have time, we are not in immediate need of the money we have invested, and we are building our future. So, it is up to us to define how much risk we can bear on our investment as we go along our journey to financial freedom. Amazing wealth has been created since the Last Great Recession 2007-2009 only 10 years ago, as investors who had built enough cash could shop around for companies who scored double- or triple-digit growth since then.

What makes absolute sense to me is that some great companies, despite crisis or recession, will still be around in 10 years and will keep growing, being true leaders in their respective sectors with a real power of disruption in the market. These are the companies I bet on and I know nothing of being a trader to venture into the unknown. I keep things simple and there can be millions of theories of what I should do or invest into or diversify into in order to do better but I am perfectly fine with the current state of affairs. I believe greed drives us to make reckless decisions with our hard earned money.

These are my comments in the present state of my understanding of my finances and the stock market, which will evolve over time as I will continue to educate myself. I will make mistakes, learn, make mistakes again, lose money/make money but this is all part of the process.

I hope that you are already well on your way towards your financial goals. If you have not yet started, how many more books do you need to read? How many more shows do you need to watch? How many more people to do you need to listen to before you take that first step and start investing?

DAY 22

My portfolio ended up practically unchanged at market close with a 60,260.30 USD value or an increase of 0.05% from the previous day. I will not spend much time, nor am I interested in the reasons why a stock picks up or drops in value day to day; this is not important to the investor who again is in it for the long term. My angle here is to share with the young investor that he/she has an unbelievable amount of time in front of him/her. The math is so simple that it does not require a degree. Should you have bought let's say an Apple share in April 2009 or 10 years ago, it would have picked up another 1300% plus or minus. Now, no one knows how much a stock price will fluctuate in the future, but the younger you start is better, and in 10 years you'll still be young, and you'll still be able to recover should the fear of losing money is the reason you have not started investing already. Simple math, a win/win situation. I believe that even if you start at 40 years old, you'll still be young at 50 nowadays, still have the time to recover any losses by the time you retire, provided you do not sell your positions and believe in the companies you have purchased.

I am trying to understand why there is so much fear wrapped around starting to invest your hard-earned money today. For my part, I have been focusing on only 4 companies since the beginning of the year, 4 companies that I have studied in and out and probably took away from my research a real 50% full understanding of all the corporate finance jargon used. Not being a financial advisor, this 50% understanding was sufficient to form my own opinion. It was even easier as I am focusing on what we call Blue-Chip companies, to add on a little more safety into my investments. Companies having the Blue-Chip status are known to have a very stable growth rate and it is considered to have less volatility than other companies that are not well established.

We are not here to become Wall Street gurus, we are here to build wealth at our own pace, by taking a few investment decisions in our lifetime, just a few investment decisions, which will be just enough to reach our goal over time, and I believe that goal is ambitious but achievable. I bought my Apple stocks at 144.02 USD a few months ago and I may have an opportunity to buy them cheaper on the next market crash probably or I may not ever see that price in my lifetime again. Just like it is highly unlikely the Apple stock price falls back to its 2009 levels at 18 USD, we will never see that happen again. If we take this angle to explain the actual value of the Apple stock in 2009, it was certainly way undervalued looking at how the company has grown since, despite what hundreds of analysts may have told you in 2009. All the possible reasons why you should not buy the stocks were outlined indeed, but should you really listen to them today, I wonder? You would not have been able to predict any of that as well as they could not. We have much more information today to play with than 10 years ago by having easier access to it and in abundance, so I strongly believe we have just raised our chances to build more wealth than ever before.

I have investments in Apple and Microsoft. I usually like blue chip technology stocks as their growth is tangible and have an immediate impact on society, right down to your own home, to our industries, to our way of life. It reassures me more than any other sectors or industry, but that's just me as I can see better what is happening and understand it better.

All of this are just examples I am giving to illustrate my thinking, I am not advising you on your investments, I can't do that but by documenting my own journey with its future successes and challenges, I am certain it will bring you the value you may need to be more confident in starting or maintaining a discipline while on your journey to financial freedom as we would be doing it together.

DAY 24

April 13th, 2019
Net Worth: 60,314.87 USD

Every day I hope we are getting closer to another financial milestone; my next milestone still remains 75,000 USD. I continue to indicate my portfolio value day to day so as to illustrate how net worth grows or depreciates overtime. It will be proof of my journey's progress in numbers for one, but also a statement I would like to make to the young, aspiring investors that all of this is not rocket science. We are sending nothing into space really, we are simply taking calculated and simple steps into building wealth.

If you did notice I have not bought a single share or sold a single share since a while. So no hard labor as well I am certainly not keeping an eye on the market during the day as I am fast asleep, since I am in Asia and my investments are in the United States. So, there is no stress here as well, I guarantee you I sleep very well as well. Why? Because I believe in the companies I have bought and in the price I have paid for them. I have ensured also to make orders to re-invest in my favorite companies should they hit certain price, just in case a market crash occurs while I sleep! That is just a matter of a few clicks on your brokerage account platform. Basically, the system will automatically buy the stock and volume at the price you have indicated, you do not even need to be present, minimal worry, minimal physical labor guaranteed. Again, all you need to do is purchase the right companies at a fair price and market will work for you.

If I had to compare my investing behavior in 2018 and 2019, it is like comparing a toddler to a grown man. I actually lost money last year from my capital, about four thousand dollars, because I acted on my emotions rather than reason, I made multiple buy/sell operations through the year, was not confident, was paying commission on each transactions, losing money, making money, just like a toddler learning to walk. I did not then give up once I posted my losses or lost faith in the stock market or myself as I took full accountability for my errors and instead of giving up, I tried again, sold everything I had with that loss and refocused my investments into my current 4 companies. I also ensured they were safer, generating dividends and since I have a history of being a very undisciplined person when it comes to money, I decided to start a podcast "The New Investor Podcast" which is my investor's conscience. It gave me a purpose, it is like a very effective therapy, as I can no longer lie to myself, people may be listening and they may get value from you, it could actually help them, or be a tiny part of why they have started to invest. Worry not of the quality of the entertainment you provide, it does not have to be perfect, what counts is the substance, the end game. This podcast will take value once I become a millionaire...and I will.... WE will.

Whatever the current state of your personal finances is or how cloudy you believe your financial future will be, both are determined by your own will to change that fate and your ability to self-start. I can assure you that the journey is an unbelievable source of happiness, as building wealth is not necessarily evaluated by the dollars but by also adding on to it new skills, a new mindset, a new purpose, a new life into you.

DAY 26

It is yet another Sunday here in Asia, and I hope you are not spending it in front of your TV or have a similar plan in mind, and that you are working on creating that other source of income with an early morning freshly brewed coffee (made at home, remember the fancy coffee story?)!

Needless to say, we are our own worst enemies, and all the ingredients are indeed together right now for you to simply let go, relax and do basically nothing today after all it is Sunday! However, I was under the impression that you dreamt to achieve your goals? I was under the impression that you were not satisfied with your present financial situation. Wouldn't then the weekend be a blessing allowing you to entirely focus on building the foundations that will support you further to reach your goals, whatever those may be? If Financial Freedom is one of them, then I believe the weekends should yield better than any other days as you are accountable to no man only to yourself and to how you allocate your time.

I strongly believe that happiness is indeed a pursuit and that it is a daily pursuit. It can be found in multiple situations, conversations, interaction with loved ones but also achievements that you have encountered in a single day. By adding them all together day by day, you would have a pretty good understanding of how to be happy.

Let me however focus on the daily achievement part, we tend to believe that we will be happy once we have achieved a major victory. I on the other hand, believe that your little daily victories will ultimately keep you happy. As an example, making a podcast episode today is for me an achievement, and it makes me happy to have been able to publish it. I was happy yesterday to have posted my previous episode and happy again the previous day which on a bigger picture brings me a lot of joy overall. To have been able to step out of my comfort zone and start something I would never thought I would do one day is simply unbelievable to me. If you take today, Sunday, to focus on your future and start or continue working on your next source of income, I am positive that by the end of the day you will feel proud of yourself and you will want to repeat that process over and over again.

If you invest on monthly basis, if you pay yourself first before considering any other monthly expense, wouldn't that be an achievement? Repeat that monthly and let me know how that feels! It is called pride, a sense of achievement added onto many others that you must continuously pursue. Should there be a market crash, wouldn't you be thrilled that you have built up some cash to buy back stocks at a discount, yes you will, and you will feel great about it. Happiness is in the process of achieving your goals. It is made up of hundreds of small victories getting you close to freedom step by step.

The road to Financial Freedom is not paved for those who think about making a quick buck or who have only money on their minds, no patience or no discipline. It is paved for Life Entrepreneurs pursuing intangibles, pursuing their own self-improvement and development, aiming at daily victories however small but while knowing that they are getting them closer to their goals.

You will inevitably change your financial situation by just applying some of the steps we outline here so that should not be a worry for you. What is of the utmost importance is that you find happiness in the process, that you are eager to step out of that couch on the weekends and find happiness while trying, while experimenting, while learning, while investing. Freewill is a powerful thing.

DAY 28

Have you already started your investing journey towards Financial Freedom? If so allow me to relay my utmost respect and admiration as you have passed the most difficult step of all, taking that leap of faith into a new world. A world that is completely foreign to you. A world that is unpredictable, probably unsafe but you have faced the Beast head on, you are therefore a warrior.

My portfolio lost value yesterday which means that it is highly probable your very first investment may have lost some value as well. This will make you feel bad or feel like you have taken a very bad decision seeing your money depleting. These are completely normal feelings of regret, failure or uncertainty about your hard-earned money. The very first reflex you will have as a first-time investor is to sell your stock quickly. Stop the bleeding and another feeling will take over. The feeling of achievement, like you have just closed a deal. A feeling of pride that you manage not to lose more than what you had already lost. What I just described is without any doubt the worst thing you could ever do while investing, acting on your emotions.

We all know that acting on emotions rather than reason in every aspect of your life have a high probability of leading to failure or disappointment. It is just like a high spending habit where you always find a romantic reason to spend your money, "I deserve it", "I worked hard for it," all the reasons you give yourself to justify your actions fueled by emotions.

As an investor, long term strategy prevails over the short-term gains. "No one wants to get rich slowly," as Warren Buffett, the legendary investor said. Nowadays, the wish for instant gratification touches deeper layers of your being. Thinking that you will build wealth quickly, retire early and travel the world…again Romance. The only thing that will happen to you quickly in this case is total failure.

To the first-time investor who has just taken that first step yesterday, have no fear, approach your journey with the long term in mind only. Believe that only patience, discipline and a strategic approach to building wealth will work out for the best, you will do well over time. Previously we covered some interesting approaches that could probably help you. I am in it with you and I will prove to you that patience and intelligent moves will lead to our success. As Charlie Munger, another wizard investor, rightfully said: "You need patience, discipline and an ability to take losses and adversity without going crazy."

What are those intelligent moves? They evidently will come to you naturally as you self-improve and you have already taken one by taking your leap of faith into investing. The second one will come with the same level of audacity and reflection.

DAY 29

If I may give a precious advice, if you absolutely must buy stocks at any point of time when the markets open, you need to avoid doing it on the first hour of trading as the fluctuations have no rationale whatsoever and it can all be qualified as a little bit of madness. The first hour is for the traders making their daily targets.

Better to wait for the markets to calm down later in the day, as to see a clearer picture and again only if you believe you could have a strike opportunity on that day. It is earnings season for a lot of great companies now and if you follow the related news, it is also a period where stock prices can be heavily affected depending on the operating results these companies have achieved in Quarter 1 2019. Analysts from major banks will create forecasts before earnings are shared by those companies and should the "earnings beat estimates", usually the stock will pick up in value and at times pretty substantially or not as a company can perform well year on year. However, one aspect of their operating results may have declined which will affect the stock price the opposite way.

Anyway, the Why is all too technical and as an investor, we have little interest in the short term. We do not live quarter to quarter, we invest today for the next 10 years or more. Should there be any Financial Analyst out there reading, this book will unfortunately not be for you as we keep it very simple here as it is in fact simple.

Analysts and TV will simply confuse you and I will highly advise you to read and research. Form your own opinion about your investing strategy and choices, rather than be influenced by multiple analysis crafted for the day or the short term on a loop all day long on those TV channels.

What forming your own opinion means? Through your research about sectors, industries and companies you are highly interested in and even passionate about, you will come across an unbelievable amount of information online to start with, coupled with the actual reports on your company's financial performance. You will also pick up books about investing, maybe I can advise you to start by reading "The Intelligent Investor" by Benjamin Graham and start your studies from there. Believe me, it is a very good start as it is an exceptional book that will serve you well and within the context.

Forming your own opinion will be about, with daily practice, creating a high degree of confidence and knowledge about a sector, a company and an industry, which will allow you therefore to invest at the right time, at a fair price while knowing your investment will have a very high probability of growing in value over time as safely as possible. You need to believe me when I say that you can already have a high degree of confidence in the US economy over time, as well as into the companies that form its pillars. You can be sure they will still be around and stronger in the future. This is simple cross analysis coupled with your own best judgement and you are smarter than you think.

A question remains, when will you start? Next time you decide to buy that next 29 dollars item, know that you can also invest in a stock, at the same price, paying you yearly dividends.

DAY 30

I would like to share some statistics and actions I have taken to prove to you what can be achieved in a short period of time by only applying determination and discipline into the projects you intend to execute, we all agree that we are working towards achieving important goals for ourselves and our future:

- **Changed spending habits**: Through rigorous savings, by changing my spending habits and by starting to invest those savings, my investment account value has grown by 2'245% since February 2018.

- **Established a Budget**: By changing my spending habits and establishing a proper budget for myself, I have managed to save 65 to 70% of my income.

- **Started Investing:** As a direct result of investing, I have realized to date 22.03% gains from my initial investment, and I am not doing anything exceptional. I last bought stocks two months ago.

- **Learned from previous mistakes and adjusted my investing strategy:** By doing this, I have increased my dividend creation from 0 USD in December 2018 to 765 USD/year only a few months later by simply investing in Blue-chip stocks (we covered BlueChip stocks in a previous episode) paying out dividends and I will only invest in stocks paying dividends. Then I will reinvest all these dividends yearly into buying more stocks

- **Increased my income in 2019:** By exceeding my target at my day to day job and unlocking my yearly bonus which in return 90% of it was used towards investing. I sacrificed, changed work location, and got promoted.

- **Launched a side Project:** I have launched a podcast and published 22 episodes to date for which I am far from being an expert on. It now has a small pool of listeners from six countries. I do this after hours and after 12 hours work days running two luxury resorts in a remote and difficult location, while ensuring I exceed my targets to increase my income.

- **Will not give up early:** I have tried and failed my first ads campaign for this podcast which ended up costing me two hundred dollars which did not convert. I learned why this could happen, readjusted, tried again by launching another campaign which could also fail but learning from my first mistake. My listeners grew from 0 to 7 in a month and my episodes played 143 times to date or 5 times on average per day. Most would qualify this as a failure due to entitlement and impatience and within the first month give up. I take this as a victory. You need to accept how the market functions and persevere as it will take years to build up an audience only IF you are good enough and IF the market adopts your what you must propose.

What is undoubtably sad, is that we tend to believe that good things or growth happens by simply wishing they did. I used to wish they did, but I certainly did not realize that so much would happen in such a short period of time by simply executing what I believe needed to be done.

DAY 33

April 21ˢᵗ 2019
Net Worth: 61,308.96 USD

The markets looks at this very instant overvalued. It is euphoric. Most of the sectors have posted double digit growth on their stocks so far, and without looking at the details here, I have a feeling that I should keep building up cash through the month of May as well. I have literally been unable to find buying opportunities this month. Everything looks expensive in my view. I was looking at some bank stocks, but they have all overpassed by far what I was ready to pay for them or judged as a fair price to pay even.

I recently stumbled upon an interesting article about how the level of wealth created in the practically immediate aftermath of the 2008 financial crisis was unprecedented. I think I have a feeling of how this happened. Many saw it coming or had a feeling that it would. They piled up cash and all went on a shopping spree on the stock market by the volume. Certainly not rocket science but in the context of investment, simply rational and smart. I will let you guess how their investments look 10 years later. The thing is, there is never enough cash to build as to be ready in the event of a stock market crash or worse. as soon as this occurs you should go out there with pure buying power. At the risk again of repeating myself as this is crucial, this is my current strategy and let's see how that evolves over time.

On another note, I am actually at the airport awaiting my flight to Bangkok. Just to give you an idea of how remote I live and work, should there be a direct flight from my location to Bangkok it would simply take 1 hour and 30 minutes. However, I should be thankful that we at least have an airport there which was not the case of my previous location. But it will take me about 12 hours to get there including a 5 hours connection wait time at the local hub. Waiting time I will of course put to good use working on my side ventures. It is amazing what can be achieved when you have time to kill and somehow airports are inspiring.

Every time I touch down in Bangkok though, I always tell myself that if I was fortunate enough to move back to such cities that I would approach my entire lifestyle there very differently. I did mention to you before how I use to spend very consistently more than 50% of my salary on things that would only bring me instant gratification with no long-term value. Now I can walk an entire mall in Bangkok and buy nothing as I now ask myself a series of question before I buy anything:

- Do I want this item, or Do I Need it?

- Will this item add value to my life?

- Would this item bring me closer to my life goals?

If I can't answer those questions with absolute certainty, then I will drop the idea. Allow me to give you an actual example. I am thinking of buying a microphone so I can increase the quality of my audio for the podcast I run:

- I Need It because I have a Podcast to run for myself and others.

- It adds value to my life because it will allow me to deliver better quality audio to anyone listening, and I will feel much better about it. I think it would add serious value to the podcast.

- It will most certainly support my intent of developing this podcast to reach a wider audience and create a community of Young and New Investors with whom we could share our respective journey towards financial freedom and support each other this way.

So it will certainly trigger a buy.
A new iPhone or iPad will not, as it will fail 2 out of 3 questions.

DAY 35

I was quite held up in the last two days as my company is currently going through our yearly Leaders' Summit and General Managers Conference coupled with workshops, team building and guest speaker. These are primarily networking events and to keep us updated on the current trends in our industry and lay out the vision for the upcoming year with a special focus on a dimension we believe will keep our competitive advantage very much alive and well. In this case they referred to being Better & Faster than our competition and the different ways we can achieve that.

I couldn't help thinking throughout these keynotes about the Young or New Investors and how it is crucial to pinpoint exactly where our strengths are and how we should double down on them rather than bringing about every effort to rectify weaknesses. We are all very good at something in particular, may it be a hobby, a creative skill, sports, a hidden gem you are yet to discover, you name it. And in this day and age we are able to potentially direct traffic, raise awareness about our product/service, monetize on all of that thanks to the power of the internet which has basically transformed everyone into an aspiring entrepreneur. It means that in order to change your life or the way you operate, it will be essential that you adapt to this new world order and evolve within it. In other words un-learn what you have learned so far and re-learn a new craft in order to survive or strive.

We are all summoned to step out of our comfort zone and evolve within that playground as this will be the only way to achieve progress. As an aspiring Young or New Investor, your comfort zone was your past life in this current world perfectly sculpted for the consumer. I was looking around the city of Bangkok (and that goes for any city), where everyone is constantly solicited to consume: you just need to walk the street to realize that everything out there talks to the consumer but nothing out there talks to the investor, why? Because it is a very different world and it was always closed to the general population. It was always there but it was a discreet world. It existed for the select few or for those who had taken the time to get acquainted to it. It was subtle. It required you to learn about it, to be curious, be diligent. It required you to take risks. It required you to learn a new language, a new philosophy of life, new values, new approaches, that is the "Outside the Box". It is the "Outside of your Comfort Zone". It is also the kind of world which as soon as you are acquainted to it, will make you feel like you have made the biggest mistake in your existence by not having been curious enough about it. We have entertained a form of arrogance that made us believe we knew better by not getting close to that world which we had defined as "not for us" but for "gamblers" or "crooks" or "for the rich". Another romantic view that only enforced our handicap and led us to build more debt rather than getting out of them.

DAY 38

I have had some very interesting days as part of my company's yearly conference. It allowed me to hold plenty of mini conversations with colleagues leading often to me talking about investing. I obviously spoke with passion and conviction as I believe this is a matter of survival in the long term. But what was quite interesting to note was the number of mature and senior leaders who are still disconnected from this world as I was. People who were, through our conversations, equally passionate about knowing more. I truly believe it is a question of lack of practical information coupled with the fear of the unknown. I was asked questions like: "Once you have started investing, how would you tackle the next financial crisis?" "Which stocks would you then advise me to buy?" "How much gains have you realized so far?"

All these questions pinpoint to a clear obsession for the short term, which is a behaviour typically associated with the consumer not the investor and I know exactly what I am talking about as I was the perfect consumer myself and for a very long time. The investor will only evolve on a playing field for the long term. While I could easily answer those questions and satisfy the person listening to me then, it is clearly a question of mindset and self-education about the subject.

We are all experts in knowing how everything functions within the consumer society; down to being able to evaluate approximate prices of goods or services, being able to compare those prices even while travelling in foreign lands, or knowing exactly how a bank loan functions. We would actively research online for the best products, trends, at the best price, at the right time. We are masters in perfecting the art of consuming. We got real good at it while being convinced that the following is why we wake up every morning: to continuously perfect our living standards by always buying more stuff, grand vacations all over Europe, 5 jackets, 7 pair of pants, 17 caps, 12 pairs of shoes, 3 phones. All of this while being completely unaware that such will lead to your personal financial failure. But wait, after all, we have entrusted our money to a pension fund or a so-called financial advisor every single month, that we will be evidently safe at retirement which in return means you can afford to enjoy your life to the fullest right away. They will, every month, tell you via a beautifully designed graph how your money will compound over time in their hands. They will tell you that the more you commit monthly the less time it will take for you to become a millionaire at the age of retirement or even 50. Of course you will, it is written right there on their brochure! You are safe, then why should you invest if "people do it for you". Should I had listened to them two years ago, I would have certainly not made the level of return I have achieved so far by self-learning the art and science of investing.

Investing is both an Art and a Science. I strongly believe that it is more Art than Science as the real return rests in your ability to deploy patience, discipline, perseverance and your ability to control your emotions, stay focused and being obsessed about the process of achieving your financial goals. Ultimately it makes you a better man or woman over time. The science can be learned but it is all about how your mind functions. It is Emotional Intelligence first and foremost.

I respect everyone's line of work. I have no personal vendetta against Financial Advisors, as it is still better than doing nothing with your money. However, I am just convinced that you can do much better by applying yourself or developing a new skillset that you never even knew you had in you. This is a form of activism that is deeply devoted to your progress. During the conference, we were asked to share with our group of colleagues "what was our greatest moment of pride". It is difficult to do so I admit, but we all managed to share an extraordinary story.

Mine? Mine happened 38 days ago when I decided to again completely step out of my comfort zone and start a podcast, being able to consistently publish 26 episodes with total plays now reaching triple digits. What was your own greatest moment of pride? It is a very valid question. Will it be today when you decide to become the artist of your own self development and take your financial future in your own hands?

DAY 39

Since these last 39 days my investment account value grew by 22.8%. It was all very simple and came down to me making only two operations:

1. I saved 68% of my salary, and

2. Re-invested 90% of my yearly bonus

The remaining increase came from the healthy start of the year on the stock market. I have not bought or sold any of my stocks since then. I did not panic. I did not give-in to my emotions when the markets opened on the negative. I did not follow any advice except my own. I was in no hurry. I remained confident about my initial choice of companies and the price I purchased them for. I started to build up cash in the event of a market meltdown and will continue to do so. I did not over diversify by going around buying up companies I do not identify myself with or highly engage with. Same goes for the sectors they evolve into. I restricted my investment into dividend growth stocks only. What I am about to say again for the hundredth time, however extremely important, regardless of your current gains, you need to be psychologically prepared to potentially lose it all in a few days while being totally unfazed by it. As Warren Buffet, the legendary investor says: "Bad news is the Investor's best friend". That will probably mean the cash you have diligently build up will come in very handy, a real buying power while wonderful companies are on a discount.

In my own personal view, feeling and opinion, should you be starting your investment journey today, the market has been on a steady growth since the beginning of the year and might be a little expensive. However, I have not scouted the whole market, nor have I been going into the details of hundreds of companies. I am talking about my own sector and companies. As an example, if you are an into biotech, are interested in that sector and instinctively follow the news on what is being done at that level and read articles on your free time, then you are probably a fan of biotech and you should then look into all the players in this sector and form your own opinion. Again, this is research, but given it is another passion of yours, it should be fun, and you will do an amazing job getting closer to these companies and end up investing in them. This is the approach; you do not have the resources investment firms have to look everywhere. Julius Caesar, Roman Emperor said: "I'd rather be first in a village than second in Rome". Given what he accomplished his advice is very valid.

If the market is at an all-time high as it is today, I would start by putting a solid saving plan and budget in place so as to focus on freeing up future investment money. Make a yearly budget, know exactly what you can spend and how much you can invest. That way, you will also see your yearly objective very clearly, this will be your goal for the year. On this one, given that we live in a society wanting everything to happen immediately, you will feel that your first-year goal may be insignificant compared to what you would need to achieve your dreams.

I have important news for you. Your plan must be a 10-year plan. If you do not have what it takes to be patient, diligent, disciplined and passionate about your own future success, I have just given you some precious information. I have just identified the root of your problem. In this case, it is a question of mindset, and that can be changed practically immediately. You are in full control.

I will share with you my current feelings about my present financial situation. I only have the macro in mind not what I have achieved so far. We are talking about Financial Freedom and that has different degrees for different people. For me, I have the past decade of being a full-on consumer to rectify. Therefore, the sky's the limit for me and that keeps me fired up while being fully aware of my achievements so far which I consider as victories.

Still reading on. Have you started your investing journey yet?

DAY 41

It is a brand-new week starting and I hope you are as excited as I am on all the possibilities that lie ahead within these seven days. I spent the weekend educating myself on digital marketing as to try and understand how to grow my new Instagram account and Website as well as other platforms, a very interesting subject indeed. I spent the weekend getting in touch with influencers to understand this all better and to possibly collaborate.

Well, one thing is certain, to receive their support for your product, service, podcast or any similar venture that requires a global presence on social media, you will need to sustain the following strategy to be relevant at least:

1. Targeted Growth

2. Content curation, viral strategies and hashtag strategies

3. Target 60 posts a month and I hear even a day across all platforms which must be relevant to your audience

4. Be active with your target audience on all platforms

5. Bring value to your audience

6. Grow your account with a high level of engagement (ideally 15% and up)

That is of course if you are already working on creating these other sources of income and such can be a full-time job. I had a feeling I needed to seek expert advice on growing my own accounts and website. I am not selling anything, just trying to raise awareness of the podcast as to possibly get closer to an ever-growing community of young or new investors. I am certainly not a graphic designer, nor a digital marketing guru. What I can tell you though is that, should you want this off your hands and have someone look after this for you with no guarantee of success, after contacting a few content curator to know more, it will cost you 1000USD per month on average!

So, to recap, in order to get started on the platforms that will support your side business, you will need:

1. Open company pages/accounts on all relevant platform to generate attention

2. Post on all platforms 2 to 10 times a day at least

3. Create meaningful content that will provide value to your targeted audience

4. Actively engage with your community

5. To not do all of this yourself, you will be asked for 1000 USD/month from a third party (money you could continue investing with a compounding effect and ultimately create buying power overtime)

The decision for me is clear and again brings us back to the same principle: put in the work. I know for a fact that the accounts for The New Investor Podcast are weak, have little followers, little engagement and will certainly not help me in their current form to grow my audience for the podcast. I will certainly not pay someone to do this for me and lose more potential to invest even if it will certainly serve me better and faster. What actions will I take?

1. I will allocate a few hours after work/before bed to actively engage with my community on social media platforms

2. I will engage with the Influencers

3. I am not a designer, so the posts will have to be relevant in a different way, maybe no need to create anything and just document. It does not have to be perfect

4. I will save the content curator salary and continue my investment journey

5. I will make my podcast better and get through to my audience on different channels

There are some very interesting materials online to teach you the ropes, again back to another principle: do your research. I am not expecting this to happen overnight but with consistency and perseverance, I have no doubt that I can double my followers and engagement within one month. That will be the target for the month of May.

DAY 42

It has now been almost 30 podcast episodes in which I have been laying out the upsides of taking your leap of faith into transforming yourself from an expert consumer into a new investor.

I was an avid consumer. I just liked purchasing beautiful things. The satisfaction of always acquiring the best or the latest was simply too great for me to just let go. I strongly believe that it was primarily driven to probably impress others due to my own insecurities. Probably linked to a need to show social status which is in any case all for the wrong reasons. The change of mindset occurred practically instantly. My wife and I got rid of 80% of our things, decluttered and gave away. The feeling once all of this was done was indescribable, a feeling of new beginnings without a doubt. The change also came with the approach I had to my finances as a whole. There was only one thing I managed to do well which was to stay out of debt. Putting myself in a position to owe money to someone or to a bank was just never part of my being. What is beyond me is that people take loans with an aim to consume more rather than to launch a business. If you have debt, you must right away start getting rid of it and whatever this may take:

- Sell your things

- Take another job

- Start a side business

The list can go on and on as there is no possible reasons nowadays, with the power of the internet in your hands, not to have multiple ways to get out of debt, but this is a priority. I understand that most of the younger population in the United States have to deal with student debt which gives you a clear handicap from the very beginning of your active life. Well, what are you going to do about it? That is the question. I spoke in earlier days on the ROI of Sacrifice or on how to grow your income. However, most people are not willing to sacrifice or work harder, while they are still sitting there wishing they had a better financial situation.

- Substantially reduce your expenses and lifestyle

- Save 50% of your income

- Pay off the debt with these extreme savings

- Do it again and again and again until this is cleared

I guarantee you one thing, once you have cleared your debt or a very large part of it, you would have already accustomed to a lifestyle that will determine your financial future. You would have as a result, learned the value of money, hard work, patience and perseverance. You would have started a side business, opened new sources of income however small, helping you further clear debt. Your objectives were clear, you were hungry to exceed them and a brand new you was therefore born. Debt is cleared, you start therefore to have disposable income. Through the pain of clearing your debt, you would have self-learned the art of investing, you would stayed curious. You would have trusted no one with your money. You would have created an ecosystem supporting you positively both in knowledge and mindset consistently.

I grew my net worth with my investments by 2 269% since February 2018, therefore it is possible, as I am no guru, and I am just like you. I just decided it was time for a change and a time to upgrade myself. If you are now the happiest person, that you are satisfied with your current financial situation, this book and the podcast may not help you much. In any other case I think it would be a good thing to follow my journey as to take your own. I plan on doubling my net worth by January 2020. I care not if that objective may seem to you unachievable and care not of what others think. Set the bar high as you are smarter than you think. You are capable of achieving all of this, whether it is clearing your debt with extreme methods or investing with extreme methods. You will be able to achieve Glory for yourself by continuously evolving outside that silly comfort zone of yours.

The objective is to double that net worth, but I have set some milestones along the way and I am close to achieving the next one and I am talking 60 days close.

What about you? When will you take charge of your future?

DAY 44

I woke up this morning pleased to see my favorite company, Apple, pick up another 4.92% in value. Very well deserved after announcing their earnings which beat estimates. That gave my portfolio a nice boost, getting me closer to another milestone I have set for myself to achieve within the next 60 days.

I believe that you should not over complicate things and that there is only a handful of wonderful business out there such as Apple, you know perfectly as they are all already part of your life.

My investments consist of 5 companies now only, carefully chosen through my own research. So far, I have followed my own judgement and purchased them all at a fair price which have proven so far to pay off. Again, I just read and studied their profile, their 10K and kept myself appraised of their news mixed with that gut feeling we never seem to follow. The gut feeling, try that, just follow each and every time it tells you to and see how that goes!

I also know that should I be following my inner greed like I did in 2018, it would end up costing me money, it is still very much alive in 2019. It is therefore important that you control these urges fueled by greed or instant gratification or the satisfaction of short-term gains. This is the reason I said that investing is more an Art than a Science because being an investor is a mindset and an attitude.

I realized that being disciplined unlocks a series of other attributes that will lead you to be successful in the long term. I will not tell you what these attributes are as the best part is when you discover them by yourself.

Start small but start. It is the beginning of the month of May and you have probably received your salary. It is imperative that you look at this income and think a different approach than last month. If you are still reading on, you have probably decided to document yourself in every possible way on how to change your current financial situation and win. I know as I did the same not so long ago. I kept consuming contents on every platform, reading every article, following every motivational speaker… you know what the secret is? Once you have started the process, you will never stop. The energy that will be created following your leap of faith will never end. By simply starting, you would have achieved 70% of your objectives already.

Look at your income this month and be very honest with yourself, can you not spare even 50 USD? Or if you have a debt to clear, are you sure you can't increase that payment by 50 or 100 USD this month? If you have disposable income and have not started investing yet, why do you work so hard then? Wouldn't this serve you better being invested in the markets or into a side business.

Possibilities are endless but you just don't know it, as fear of the unknown prevails still. You have not decided to face the beast yet. I understand, as I have not faced it until my mid 30's. Believe me I am you, the beast is you, it is your fear, your apprehensions, your ego, your arrogance, your consumerism. It is everything that prevents you from taking another path that is actually filled with contentment, continuous sense of achievement, happiness, peace of mind, pride, knowledge, and self-development. A path that will simply lay the first stones of you becoming a better man or woman.

Once you have set your sights on let's say clearing your student loan fast and have taken all the disposition to do so, with the level of sacrifice it requires, and you actually managed to clear an additional 5% of that debt you usually never contemplated with your current lifestyle, let me know how that feels. It is called a moment of Glory not just a victory. Repeat again and again, clear that terrible burden the system has imposed on you as you have other fish to fry, do it now, do it early. You just got paid, review carefully what you will do with this money as of today and every month, and take action to increase your income right away.

DAY 46

It is amazing what can be achieved in a week with even measurable results. As I mentioned before, the important is achieving progress towards your objective however small the steps you are taking are. I am extremely pleased of my own results this week after putting in the work. They are not the sexy results compared to your idols but please do not compare yourself to others, be yourself, do you. Those you admire have been doing this for years already and we are just starting the journey.

Please do not tell me you do not have the time or that you are too busy to focus on your progress towards financial freedom, the achievements I have scored this week are on top of me leading a team of 160 people and running two busy luxury hotels:

- Increased my account value by 8.6% through capital gains and by reinvesting 55% of my income. Getting now very close to my next milestone. My net worth increased by 2,592% since February 2018. This is what you can achieve by simply starting today. Take the weekend again to reflect, reflect and reflect again... Face the Beast on Monday

- Increased my cash position as promised. I invested it all into the S&P 500 ETF (SPY) yesterday however, with a stop loss (you set your own limit, system will sell your position once reached) set at

1.5%. This is only to ensure I benefit from any upsides; ensure I do not lose much as well as make sure my cash does not just sit there. I detail why I am building up cash previously.

- Learned how to run ads on LinkedIn to generate some traffic on The New Investor Podcast's website. Ads failed two times, tried again, refined it and is now giving some satisfactory results. Not good enough though, I will have to study this further. Looking at the stats, that type of ad is actually very cheap given the number of people you reach within your target audience. I don't how long that will last but take advantage of it until a click costs you 20 USD or more. By the way, I sell nothing. My content is free so far, so these are pure expenses. I believe you should stop wanting to monetize everything way too early in the process.

- Set myself an objective to double followers and engagement by the end of May and working on it.

- Published 5 episodes of the podcast, I want to thank everyone for listening as the audience has grown to a slightly wider group now from all over the world.

My point here is that there are numerous angles that I have taken to grow. This whole process of getting to your goal is such an excitement that you do have endless energy. There are real moments of happiness. I have a feeling that I am on the right path so far, so I will double down on all of this.

I will tell you what I did not do this week which I should have done better:

- I did not engage with the investor's community and influencers enough on Instagram which has affected my progress towards my month of May goal, to double my followers and engagement on this platform. By the way, make no mistake about it, in our day and age you must stay relevant and present on these platforms to exist as an entity trying to grow your service or business. Even if it is free.

DAY 47

478 days since I have taken my first steps towards a brighter financial future. Through this single most important move, my life has radically changed. I invested my first 2,600 USD; it was also the minimum I required to open that brokerage account. For an expert consumer like me at the time, it was hard to let go of such buying power. Therefore, I immediately started to lose money. Markets in the first few months of that year were slow and I did not research or studied the companies I had purchased. Just going with the flow and I lost 500 USD in April 2018. I got my hopes back up, then making good gains after reviewing my investment style mid-year, until Christmas Day, my portfolio value then lost more than 5,000 USD. However, the point here is that while I made some irrational decisions based on emotions throughout that year buying high selling low, listening to the news and other people's opinions, changing my strategy 3 or 4 times. I did not give in to those emotions to give up entirely or sell off everything, losing faith and returning to being that expert consumer. I learned the meaning of discipline in financial planning as I consistently re-invested large portions of my income every single month, reduced my expenses by 70%, established a solid yearly budget which allowed me to almost meet my yearly objective which I met a month later due to unplanned expenses.

Believe me, by creating a structure around you that you commit on following, things become magically easier and your feeling of accomplishment is constant, you are simply happier. The same technique applies if you must clear debt on top of this. This is no rocket science, it just requires will and determination to change your financial outcome and even change as a person. There is nothing in this plan that would drastically change your life. You will just learn to live differently and with less as well as only consider acquiring or doing things that bring true value to you or your life. In the meantime, that 1000 USD you would have invested this month could compound at 7% yearly for 10 years turning into more than 200,000 USD. Why are we committed to working so hard to make that 1000 USD and not courageous enough to put it aside as investment?

In 2018, I learned key principles that have already determined, I believe my entire future, and I am still learning, these are my feelings about them:

- Patience: I believe you should not be in a hurry to make a quick buck. Do not be a short-term player, you will lose. Make the right choices through research, curiosity, apply yourself in deep diving into companies you love and understand. Then you can strike. A single good strike can change your entire future.

- Perseverance: do not give up, never give up. The inner voice telling you to stop, which used to live in me last year, is telling you exactly what you should not do. Keep at it, the fight is exciting and tremendously rewarding. If you believe this is hardship you may be wrong, some people in this world do have it worse than you do.

- Discipline: I believe by establishing a system for yourself that you do not deviate from no matter what will do the trick. I do not waste time. As soon as I receive my income, I go ahead and make all necessary operations from day 1.

- Investing in yourself: even the bit of knowledge acquired during the journey has served me better to make decisions and to maintain all of the principles I outlined. I developed a strong belief that the human being has more hidden talents than those that are fully exposed.

- Keep evolving: where the air is rarified, our hidden talents are real power. To discover them, you must evolve outside your comfort zone in everything you do. Those talents are perfected over time if you stay in that zone long enough.

- Accept challenges you normally would not take: to be very honest with you, I never thought I would do a podcast on investing. I was the perfect consumer, never invested a dime in my life. I am not a radio host, I make mistake while I speak, English is my second language! Take a challenge you would normally never take.

By the way, I think all of this; the investing, the complete change of mindset, the thirst for knowledge, the quest for victory and even glory, launching your side business is a translation of our deepest wish to pursue happiness in all its forms.

By having tested and tried happiness through instant gratification for so long, I can tell you that I am today happier than ever before as I stepped onto this new path towards financial freedom.

DAY 48

May 6th, 2019
Net Worth: 66,739.28 USD

I wanted to spend some time on how I will face the most recent news that President Trump will consider imposing additional tariffs on trade with China, which also possibly means that we are nowhere close to a bilateral accord between these two nations on that subject. China markets opened at -4% and currently hitting -6%. S&P 500 Futures signals that the markets will open on the negative probably close to 2% and the Nasdaq 100 close to 2.25%. These will weigh on my gains so far for sure but don't forget that we have been on a steady growth for a very long time and that the S&P 500 already hit an all-time high. So unless you are powered by insatiable greed, I am sure you will be able to survive this news. The way I see it and the important point here, is not to cede to panic and start to sell off, as no investor cares about the day to day, only the macro matters evidently.

Only yesterday, I did say that I had parked my cash in the S&P 500 as to benefit from any upsides. Well that is going to be short lived.

When such a news occurs, I usually keep an eye on the companies I have placed on my watchlist and hope they will hit the fair price I had in mind. If so, I will certainly start shopping around. Let's see on the open if this news triggers a good enough dip in the markets for me to start shopping. If not, then I will not and just wait until all of this pass. I have some forward planning ideas in terms of my next investments which is always a good thing to do.

In those times, however serious in their degrees, I am sure you now realize the importance to always have cash on hand. Feeling like you are benefiting from markets downsides or bad economic news, means you are benefiting from all the possible dynamics of the market, may they be positive or negative. It is a good feeling to have and I believe that is always a good way to go.

I was informed today that another smaller bonus from a past property I was managing last year had been approved, which means I will be receiving additional funds that I did not forecast. Don't call it luck as the fruits of your hard work are deserved to you and only you know the level of commitment you have deployed to increase your income through performance at your current job. We did speak about how to grow your income, this is how it is done and I am obviously thrilled about it as it could come at an opportune time.

I will be able to unfortunately invest only 50% of it as life at times will bring essential expenses to your attention which you must commit to and which I can now to attend to earlier on in my agenda, which is great. As you can see, regardless, I am still able to commit a percentage to investment. You should always commit a percentage to your future self, always, even if you have debt to clear.

I read a recent article outlining that 42% of Americans have only 10,000 USD saved for their retirement, that basically means retiring poor, in stress, in need and that is not America. I would do anything to have a chance to live and work in the United States, as seen from where I am today, it is the land of opportunities without a doubt. 42% of Americans should be retiring with a million dollars and we are here to do exactly that. Let's push this a little, a million will be only one of our milestones.

To recap:

- Don't panic.
- Keep an eye on your watchlist if you have cash on hand.
- This is just one news and there is no reason to worry for the future of the US economy in 10/20 or 30 years.

- Only if and it is a big IF, companies hit the fair price you have determined to pay then go out there and start shopping. I will do nothing if this does not happen, but that's just me taking my own decisions based on my own best judgement.

- If you happen to have cash sitting somewhere, invest a percentage of it or park it into cash for the purpose of investment.

DAY 49

May 7th, 2019
Net Worth: 65,996.00 USD

As you can probably judge, what has started as a bad day on the stock market following the news from the White House on further tariffs on Chinese goods, ended up looking like any other regular day with losses indeed but not really should your investments remained unchanged since the beginning of the year. My portfolio lost 0.92% in value, hardly anything exceptional if your aim was to take advantage of that news to shop around for companies. However, when the markets opened, you could have easily given in to your emotions and started following everybody with their sell offs. I hope you have not and if you did I hope you have learned something new!

The ideal attitude to adopt however, is to never look at your investments until it is 2030. There is no need for you to look at them if you are confident you have made the right moves in the first place. The real purpose, for me at least, is to keep learning what affects the dynamics of the markets, how these influence my investments, how news affects my investments in the short term. I am also training my mind to remain disciplined and walk my talk, a good self-development technique. So I look at my investments every day and for 2 hours before I go to sleep and forget about them until morning, when I then pick up my phone and give a last look for the day. I am not afraid of the markets melting overnight as I have set my "stop losses" to dooms day mode. Meaning that I set my losses to the level of risk I am ready to accept should the financial crisis occurs while I am fast asleep (I live in Asia, just as a reminder, with opposite time zones).

What is going through my mind these past few days is how I should have started my investing journey earlier. I will blame no one but myself but I have been meaning to say to those who have not yet started, that the longer you wait, the more regret you will build along with your years. I wonder how many more pieces of contents you need to consume on the subject before making your first steps. Which word or seminar or book or podcast or article or TV show will be the one that will change your life? Do you really need all that sound and visual effect, decors, glossy book cover, or a renowned writer or top of the charts podcasts to build up your confidence further to act, I remind you, on your own future? Why would the word *start* not be enough?

Creating a podcast or a book perfectly beautified to fit the consumer is by no means an intention here and I do not know how to run such a show. The objective is not to entertain you but to tell you the truth. There will be no ads, no courses, and no group coaching sessions to sell you, just pure thoughts and documenting the experience from a young investor on his path to another. The podcast will grow organically for those who seek practical approaches to start investing, build wealth and I will add gaining the right mindset to basically succeed in any aspects of one's life.

I document the day to day, and that will include the money, the worries, the challenges, the concerns that a young investor is going through, not words from a billionaire to a young crowd. The question I now ask myself is, why, would I spend time doing that instead of simply focusing on the path? Because it is part of my own process and I am obsessed by it not by the end game. It is getting me closer to my goal as this podcast and this book acts as my investor's conscience to keep walking my talk and stay disciplined but deep inside having high hopes it will bring value.

DAY 51

May 9th, 2019
Net Worth: 64,704.77 USD

In the last few days, my portfolio value dropped by almost 3%, no cause for concerns as I am way up since the beginning of the year. The important thing here is not to lose money on your initial investment. I have been watching closely as one company stock price is slowly approaching the threshold I am ready to pay, my only wish at the moment is that markets keep on dropping in the next few days. I am convinced however that this US-China trade war situation will reach a compromise at some point. Should this happen, you will most certainly see further gains on your portfolio. Watch and see.

My point here is that investing is all about Patience to grab the right opportunities. If you are going to hold a stock for 10 or 20 years, it is ok to take your time making the right choice both in company and price. How to do that? This is where you will need to do some homework and start researching the companies you are seeking to acquire, here is what you need to look for:

- Industry and Sector: Is this company evolving in an industry or sector you are highly interested in, even passionate about?

- Company: Is this a company you are already using product or services from? Are you inspired by their vision and mission? Do you see this company being a major player in the next decade? Is this company too big to fail? Does it have a very solid competitive advantage in all its aspects?

- News: personalize your news app to feed you all the news out there about the company, the industry or sector. Form your own opinion on the company's image, cross examine all the information you have gathered with an aim to form that definite opinion. You will need to keep following them, as they continually change or adapt to remain competitive, better and faster or know if they are starting to be less relevant on the market. These are quite abstract I admit, but I say it again, Investing is rather an Art than a Science.

- Financial Reports: you will then need to dig into the numbers and as listed companies, all of their financial information is available through their website in the Investor's Relations section. I personally read their 10K which is their yearly financial performance report which outlines all the information allowing you to determine how solid a company is.

- To better understand that report, I simply started reading it and whenever there was a term I did not understand, I simply researched it. I researched terms I did not understand within the terms I did not understand. Consumed content on the terms I did not understand and how they apply in corporate finance or into the context of my understanding. This is how I developed a better understanding, not a full understanding but enough to form an opinion and reinforce my confidence into the company.

- Quarterly Earnings Call: Every quarter these companies will hold their Q review calls in presence of financial advisors also shareholders in the company, will answer some Q&A but overall will present their figures. This is a great way to get to know from afar the management, their strategy or thinking behind what led to their performance, or what led to increasing or decreasing the value of the company. This all brings a little more color into your research and a nice way to develop your understanding of corporate finance.

There are multiple ways to determine the right price at which you should buy the stock and believe that is a question everyone in that world is usually trying to figure out. Some of the best investors out there have at times bought companies overpriced, this is not an exact science. My question is, what is the harm in building cash and simply waiting for a major market correction or crash before buying up the companies you love? They will all be offered at a discount; you will not have to worry too much about striking a bull's eye.

DAY 53

May 11th, 2019
Net Worth: 68,537.03 USD

The past week has been filled with learning opportunities in addition to putting to the test our ability to remain composed and calm in the face of uncertainty and the dangers from a trade war between the US and China that could become uncontrollable and ultimately dangerous for the world economy. The markets have reacted to the news pretty sharply creating some buying opportunities which I hope to have occurred for the companies on your watchlist. If not, I must then commend you on your patience and composure, you could have succumbed to your emotions and started selling off your companies. Let's have a look at the reasoning behind this for a moment, begin by asking yourself these questions:

- Would you sell your home if you had a flood this morning? You would certainly not.

- Would you sell your shop if you had a single bad sales day? You would certainly not.

It is important to take actions which are proportionate to events and I believe a headline is not a reason to sell your companies as you are holding them for another 10 to 20 years or even forever so there will be plenty of those headlines along the way. These headlines or occasional setbacks are normal and the only thing they should spark is buying opportunities. We are not in the business of selling our companies. We are in the business of buying great companies and businesses. The companies you have purchased were purchased because of very valid and calculated reasons at a particular time and price, because you were convinced that they will still be around in 10 years and that they will continue to do well. As far as I am concerned, this week has allowed me to increase my position in one of my companies and buy another at the stock price I had in mind and I wish I had more cash on hand to buy more of them. On the previous days, we did focus on the importance of building cash up to ensure you maintain a strong buying power in case headlines or a market crash occurs.

We look at the price of stocks not at the news. Bad news will allow for the stocks you are eying to become buying opportunities. Regarding the price of the stocks, there are multiple ways to value stocks to determine what would be the best price possible. It is not an exact science as everyone is trying to work this out and everyone has a theory or a number. I prefer to look at the value of the business, both in their tangibles and intangibles, rather than the stock price and you'll be able to judge if the price you are paying for it is fair or not. I am of the thinking that over time you will do well, provided you have selected the right companies to own.

There could be exceptional circumstances that could occur over a period of 10 years or more that will force you to sell, as a company can actually fail. What I have done is complete two steps first:

- I determine the level of risk I can take, given my present personal financial situation. Basically, how much money am I comfortable losing through an investment?

- I set up what we call "stop losses" according to these risks and determine the percentage I am ready to lose so as to give a chance to the stock to bounce back.

Should the market drive the stock price below, the system will automatically sell my stock at the price I would have set. Such would allow me to forecast as well my "worst case scenario", which is a good way to always know where I stand or could stand with my investments in any circumstance. These are all things I personally do which work well for me. I have made my purchases on Thursday and Friday, which means that I have waited out for the news to be digested by the markets. I observed before that bad news will affect the markets with day by day declines, so better to wait for the declines to reach their peak before making your moves. As far as I am concerned, I am satisfied with my purchases and should they decline further in their price so be it, we are not investing billions so a dollar or two won't make a huge difference, just be confident that you have purchased the right company.

DAY 55

May 13th, 2019
Net Worth: 68,477.17 USD

I hope you have had a great weekend and for those who listened my last episode The Saturday Debrief, it looks like the upcoming week on the markets will reflect the continued tensions between the US and China, currently negotiating a possible trade agreement. This morning futures overall were down on average 1%, that means that we should expect the markets to open on the negative today. Good news for the investors who still have their eyes on their watchlist this week.

As far as I am concerned, I have no plans to make any financial operation as I have made all of them already. I bought the companies I wanted to buy at the prices I considered as fair. My only strategy moving forward is to keep building cash until another shopping day occurs, may be this year, maybe not, maybe in 2020 who knows. There is absolutely nothing wrong with building up cash and parking it in the S&P 500 with a stop loss of 1.5%. I will do this once my cash reserves have been refilled in the next few months. My portfolio now consists of 5 companies, my asset allocation is as follows

1. Apple 42%

2. Bank of America 26%

3. My current Company, a Major Hospitality Group 17%

4. Microsoft 8%

    5.   JP Morgan & Chase 7%

There are also one thousand theories on what is the best asset allocation you should adopt. I believe this one is based on the level of risk I am able to bear, based on my present financial and life situations, my age - as the younger you are and probably the more risk you can take as you have time to recover. The theory is that you will do well overtime, anyway, provided you invest in the right companies.

Investing in the right companies is easier said than done, that is correct, but please refer to my own list. I am not venturing into the unknown, I am staying somewhat safe in my choices. A few things came out while researching these companies and this is my own point of view, I could be wrong:

1.   They have all resurfaced stronger from a major crisis.

2.   They are all disruptors in their own sectors.

3.   They all have a sustainable ability to maintain competitive advantage over their competitors which makes it difficult to wear down their market share.

4.   They all pay dividends.

5.   They will all be around and strong in 10/20 years, even further than that. They all could disrupt the market in the foreseeable future, and I like that.

6.   Strong leadership team.

7.   Solid Brand Equity.

8.   3 of the 5 are recent major holdings of Mr. Warren Buffett's (Being who he is and judging from what he has accomplished, don't argue, call a chicken a chicken, these companies are good enough for your dollars). Them being recent acquisitions allows you to get good data on the price he may have acquired them for, even if he does so with preferred shares usually at a better price.

There are multiple other reasons mainly related to these companies' finances that are important without a doubt, but I can't spend time on something I have only halfway knowledge about. However, I believe that having these 8 attributes are to me solid reasons to have looked at them in the first place.

I want to outline that you really do not need to be an expert to start investing. I remain simple in my approach. There are 250,000 podcasts and even more books out there on Investing with acute and advanced analysis on the market, ratios and indexes that are here for the trader to make short term decisions to make a profit, and we are not burdened by this. We are looking 10 or 20 years in the future, not tomorrow.

People with over-diversified portfolios and hundreds of millions of dollars invested, have teams they pay millions a year to gather data for them and even they do not beat the market. What makes you think we will with our level of resources?

My theory is that I may have already substantially changed my financial future in one way or the other with the 5 companies I have already bought today.

DAY 56

As predicted, the week will be filled with opportunities for the investors who are waiting a little longer for further dips in the market to start shopping. So far, 2 full months of gains have been wiped out my portfolio value and this will continue this week for sure. I am still up full year by 9.33% but that will not last today or in the coming days should the trade war tensions escalate further. No one would like to see an escalation as such, as there are serious and unforeseen under courants that could harm the world economy. That would be an entire different story to tell here. In the meantime, those who have cash on the side can seriously start thinking of using it for one of those companies on their watchlist.

Despite all these turmoil in the markets, I will not sell or rethink my approach as this can be a costly mistake. We all know that that one news is the main factor of these dips and the markets will rebound, as it usually does for the past centuries and even stronger, once tensions have been relieved with an actual agreement signed between the US and China.

However, you do not need to worry about that. You do not need to ask yourself so many questions or try to predict the "if's". Your lifetime will be made of countless headlines that will affect your investments but that is entirely part of the game. We can talk about that further in 10 years but in 10 years you would have done very well for yourself at least better than not investing at all.

I do not believe it is important that you managed to buy a stock one dollar cheaper than me or that we should have waited a little longer to get the perfect discount. I believe the important thing is that you have placed your trust and confidence into a wonderful business, that you now partially own, which will continue to strive along with the US economy and that you will get great returns in a decade because you most certainly will. It is a fact; most people lose on the stock market for forfeiting their ability to be patient, for wanting to be rich quick, which is the quickest way not to. As I said before, those who have started investing today, who are willing to sacrifice, be patient, disciplined and resilient, work hard on every fronts to grow their income, save big and invest big monthly, live with little and not care how they are judged; those young or new investors have already changed their financial future. Some have already made the move that will make them rich in the next decade or two.

My personal feeling when I saw these sell offs in the market in volume is how little faith there is in the companies that make up the strongest economy in the world and how much fear and greed prevails on the stock market. What I also see is tremendous opportunities being created from chaos, which I hope you are also seeing, that you have that hard-earned cash ready to enter the market if you have not already done so.

DAY 58

I think the recent fluctuations on the markets are statements reminding me of valuable traits to uphold as an investor, the immense value of discipline, the virtue of patience but I would also add trust and confidence in my choices.

As an investor, selling off your company is a statement of distrust in your own choices, in the men and women leading and forming the organization you have invested in and a lack of understanding of the history of the stock market that has basically emerged stronger from every single mega crisis that ever occurred. The only variable you must be sure to control as much as possible is the companies you chose to invest in, and again they are evident to me as I keep things very simple. I always like to refer to Mr. Warren Buffett, the legendary investor also called the Oracle of Omaha, who I believe putting aside the qualities making him earn his reputation. If you have a look at only the Top 5 of his company's equity holdings, which represent almost 64% of his total portfolio:

1. Apple

2. Bank of America

3. Wells Fargo

4. Coca Cola

5. American Express

What do we notice in the simplest of forms? That Mr. Warren Buffett invest in companies that you very well know, that you consume every day and that have a very solid brand equity all over the world. These are all major companies, blue chip companies. He did not venture in territories that he did not understand or that did not have widely available and rich historical data.

My point is, I believe that at the present time I should keep my investments decisions simple, grounded and realistic. There are without a doubt, start-up companies out there which will disrupt the way we live. Being a tech enthusiast myself, I have my own vision of what the world will be in the next 10 or 20 years. I follow advancements in technology with all sectors but this will certainly not mean I will invest in BioTech or Artificial Intelligence or Robotics today as such moves do not fit my investment philosophy on the present day. I have no will to pursue on getting rich fast, or make that killer move with the current state of my net worth as this has the potential to ruin you fast.

The plan is to build wealth first, reach a level of financial independence that would allow you to invest "for fun" on the side in such sectors with a higher level of risk or companies shaping the future, that will take time to achieve but it is my goal as I am passionate about it, and for that you need a solid net worth and time.

I propose that you take your dream as well as financial goal and engineer the whole process of getting there backwards. Establish a strategy that you will not deviate from no matter what through discipline, sacrifice and hard work. Believe it or not, the first step in achieving your dreams does have an Investment strategy as a major step forward. The beautiful thing that occurs is that once you have started investing and building your net worth, you can no longer stop building it. You start seeing clearly how to get rid of all and any financial burden, how to save and invest, you start learning, reading, planning, creating. Everything becomes possible because you suddenly have a purpose. You start being passionate about the whole process of reaching Financial Freedom. You will no longer do this for the money as you would have understood how money is made.

DAY 59

Recovering slowly from the past week and that still does not matter to me or to the investor. I am sure you have by now figured out how emotional the market can be. We like it to stay this way, as such offers multiple opportunities during the year to make our moves. Bear in mind that the upcoming elections in the US in 2020 will bear more headlines affecting the markets, so I will keep building cash until then.

I received by Apple dividends payment yesterday, 111 USD, a nice number and I am sure the first thing that came to your mind is how small that quarterly payment is compared to the investment I have made. Allow me then to explain why I have chosen my investment strategy to focus only on companies paying dividends. While that number from Apple may appear small, should I currently add up the dividend's payment from all my companies at the current stage of my portfolio, I would receive in 2019, 1'120 USD before tax. The other angle I wish to take is through the investments I made last week following the US-China Trade War headlines. I created another 356 USD per year worth of dividends. I had 0 dollars at the beginning of 2019 in terms of dividends or additional income, I believe we must perpetually build wealth and investing in stocks that are highly volatile and offer no dividends is a mistake I made in 2018 and I ended up losing money. Looking at 2019 performance, I have without a doubt found my long-term strategy.

You may find that 66 USD/month after tax from these dividends on average is not going to make you rich, but I trust and hope that the mindset of getting there quick has already left your body. What scares me the most is making rushed decisions on an objective of this magnitude. I built up these dividends in 6 months, but the process to be able to free up investment money to get to these 66 USD is where the work is, the hardship and the sacrifice. Make no mistake about it as well, it will take me years to build dividends that are substantial enough to at least cover a percentage of my life expenses. That is another goal but I will reinvest all my yearly dividends every year into more stocks or "free" stocks which will allow my account value to compound. I feel that this is again a wise, structured and viable approach to build wealth over time.

Through the podcast and the book, I will be transparent on every move that I make as I believe there is no better way than to share the truth of a journey that will take me years. What I am excited about is hundreds of episodes and chapters down the line that I will be able to go back to this one with a very different net worth and prove that anyone can do this. Anyone can change their future provided they are not in a rush leading them to make dumb decisions with their money, that they have stayed the course, grown their income, lived with little and got rid of all bad debt. This is my future, the future Me must be able to thank the present Me for all he did, not curse Him.

I don't know about you but what scares me the most is to be filled with Regret. If I had to talk about regret, not starting to invest already 10 years ago is my biggest one and I already feel regret down to my bone. I can't even begin to imagine what regret feels like when you are 65 years old and you have nothing.

Knowing this, my approach now is to make up for the time I have lost, which will require double efforts on my part. This is my cross to carry and once this is fixed, I will drop it and never think of it again.

Bill Gates said something very true, along the lines that if you are born poor it is not your fault but if you die poor it is entirely your fault.

He did not simply refer to money. It also means that you would have taken full ownership of your future, changed your situation with drastic solutions, educated yourself to give you the necessary tools for success, worked hard to grow your income, been creative to open new sources of income, probably failed along the way many times but by knowing the alternative you got up again and marched.

It is an attitude, a mindset and a way of life. I am far from my goal; I will fail multiple times, but I am so glad that I will, as this is exactly what will make me successful.

DAY 62

May 20th, 2019
Net Worth: 66,646.30 USD

I kept a little busy this weekend, revamping my website. I linked the podcast to it and relooked at the design and functionality, quite simplistic still but I will get better at it.

There are some very user-friendly tools out there at low cost which can enable anyone to actually set up an online presence easily. In a matter of a few weeks, I learned to create a website, learned more about Search Engine Optimization, learned more about running ads online to direct traffic to the website, learned how to create infographics for Instagram posts. While I am not an expert at this, I will continue to apply myself and the knowledge will compound over time just like your investments! I also believe there are no longer any valid excuses to at least trying to be successful as all the knowledge is practically free. I will therefore question your will.

I am not selling anything, so it is just there for all to follow if ever I do a good job in bringing some value to you while deciding or already fully engaged in your investing journey.

I am very much looking forward to this week on the markets. It will be interesting to see how the US/China Trade dispute develops and for how long. 11 days to go before pay day, hope there will be further opportunities should this soft crisis stretch a little longer and that my hard-earned money can go towards investments.

I plan on injecting 58% of my salary next month, up from 55% last month. I am sharing here that I am determined to be consistent in my investments on a monthly basis and no matter what. I am sure that if like me you start auditing where your expenses go to, it is with certainty that I tell you that you will find areas where you can save further. I considered drastic changes in my lifestyle down to the coffee I drink. Doing a 360-degree audit of your spending circle and acting on it while accepting a serious level of sacrifice and not caring how others may judge you, will actually change your life. That is real.

I just read that a billionaire has decided to take care of the student debt of 400 students and some had amassed $200,000 worth of student loan. I believe this is a tragedy to allow the young generation to start off in life with such a handicap, but if you are one of them, your only objective must remain to clear this off, whatever it takes. I have worked with people leaving family and friends to work on higher wages in remote locations to save all their income to pay off debt or build their future. I think people are generally not willing to sacrifice. I believe that the ability to sacrifice and take steps to better your situation, whatever the cost of your comfort may be, will allow you not only to clear off any debt faster than you can even conceive but also develop a mindset set on winning mode. Everything will become clearer and you will change the outcome of your life once you understand the value of sacrifice.

I understood the value of sacrifice since I was 19 years old through my career in difficult parts of the world. I did not understand the value of money though until only recently once I took my leap of faith into investing. Make no mistake about it, once you have understood both the value of Sacrifice and the value of Money, there will be very little standing in your way to financial freedom.

DAY 65

A few words on the markets which have been up and down lately, to summarize, my investments have not been picking up much to recover from a 12% drop in gains since the beginning of the month. All of this does not matter, what matters is that you do not lose money on your initial investment.

A 6 or 7% gain by the end of year is perfectly acceptable. Just ensure you keep increasing your account value through your consistent monthly investments. Make sure you achieve your savings goal every month for that exact purpose. As far as I am concerned, not reaching my next financial milestone is not an option. I am laser focused. It will be reached, and it will be history as I will be focusing on the next one and it will feel fantastic.

Today I will post multiple articles on my website and ensure the most researched words on the net within my topics are found in each of these articles. I would like to increase my chances that my website be found on Google or search engines (otherwise called SEO), redirect traffic and attempt to increase the audience for the podcast. I am, however, humbled that the number of subscribers is increasing and that I can be a tiny part of your mornings.

I have been focusing on finding ways to increase my podcast audience and my website traffic for the last few days and I must say that there is again an abundance of content to teach you how to do that. I realized that, while extremely undervalued and extremely powerful, LinkedIn advertising started to cost me quite a bit of money for no possible conversion as I am not selling any products or service, so I have paused them indefinitely. I have placed a bet however on another ads provider which I pay less than 40 USD a month and while website traffic is cut by half on daily basis, it will run for a full month, at a fraction of the price. I believe that once you cut down your expectations of believing that everything you do must go viral or else is not worth it and be happy with 15 people visiting your website with a low bounce rate, see this as a victory and again all of this will compound over time just like your investments!

I have secured the advertising at a low cost with a good enough reach for me 5 days ago and the website has been visited 114 times with a bounce rate of 60% (means just a click, not visiting etc.). If I can covert as low as 5% to keep listening to the podcast, I will consider this as tremendous progress. This is exactly how you should look at your investments or your savings. A succession of small victories will lead you to reach ambitious goals but for this to occur, you need to recognize them.

Believe that saving an additional dollar a day is a victory, save 1 dollar a day for 30 days, you save 30 dollars/month or 360 USD per year. With 360 dollars you can purchase 13 shares of Bank of America which will generate a dividend of 8 USD/year. Shall I continue? A coffee serving is 0.36 ounces or 10 grams. A jar of instant coffee is 50 gram will cost you approximately 8 USD. That one dollar saving a day will therefore cover your reasonable daily coffee consumption for almost 2 months. Try an apply the same reasoning to all your current expenses and see where are the low hanging fruits that you can tackle right away and those that you can achieve in a short, medium or long term.

Others will classify you as "stingy". I would classify you as a smart forward-looking investor well on his way to financial freedom. I like that one much better. Most of the actions we take are predicated on how others may perceive us or judge us as a result. Allow me to remind you that we are talking about your financial future, ultimately your survival, your happiness, your security and your freedom. That should be enough for a reply like, "I don't really care what you think, I am sure you have enough to deal with on your own".

DAY 66

I came across this morning, a very interesting pattern, on the number of listeners of the podcast. The graph is closely correlated with the market movements. When markets do well my podcast does well and much less when the contrary would occur. However, the average listening time increases, boosted by the beloved subscribers base.

I believe this is interesting as the overwhelming majority of people would entertain a strong belief that they should start investing when markets are trending positive, again motivated by short term goals. Whereas, I can assure you that to start investing today when the markets are trending on the negative would be an excellent move for the long term. Should I look at my companies right now, they are all trading on a very interesting discount and I believe the upcoming few days could be a very good time to start your journey.

For those who have committed already, just be patient. I have no other tips to give you. Stop thinking about those guys who are currently acquiring stocks cheaper than you did, they do not matter as the majority of them will sell them as soon as they can make a profit. Not you, you will look at your gains in 10 or 15 years. What you could do now if you have cash on hand is to increase your positions in your current companies to lower your average further, a good way as you would increase your dividends yield at the same time, a win-win.

What am I looking at? I have my eyes currently on Apple. While being my largest position, I can't wait for the stock to drop at Q4 2018 levels. It seems well on its way as 17% of their revenue comes from China. Their next quarterly earnings will happen in July and should the US-China tension keep the momentum, in addition to the expected drop in their top line revenues and profits as a result, I might as well get an opportunity to lower my average for my favorite stock. There will be nothing stopping me building cash until then, the opportunity seems promising. As you can also judge, I look at no other sector, no other stock, no other trend but the companies I love and understand. There is no need and when the opportunity occurs, I will go all in.

I am less than 10,000 USD away from my next milestone. I was closer not so long ago but it is best not to count on pure capital growth when you build wealth but rather on your ability to inject more capital, through diligently creating disposable income for the purpose of investments. Such is achieved through successfully re-engineering yourself and adjusting to a lifestyle that will fully supports this.

I would like however to be clear, you oversee the organization of your life. There are three important things in life I believe, such as health, relationships and wealth. There are two pillars Health and Relationships that come before Wealth and your level of commitment to them are paramount for the third to ever happen. Ask yourself what you are currently doing to improve all three.

For my part, the coming week will focus on Relationships. I will be in Singapore on a last-minute business trip as of Sunday for the full week and I will be travelling with my lovely wife who is believe me very much looking forward to leave our current location for a few days as I am. I will refer you back to earlier days and our talks about Sacrifice.

DAY 71

May 30th, 2019
Net Worth: 64,840.09 USD

The last few days in Singapore were eye opening for me on many levels. It was very interesting to observe the high volume of travel industry and hospitality professionals reflecting, gathering statistics, booking trends how/where/when the millionaire travelers from Asia are currently looking at in terms of their destinations preferences, type of hotels and what experiences and services we need to propose to ensure we as hoteliers are able to catch their attention and you guessed it… make them spend their money!

However, the industry is still harmless as we sell fantastic accommodation in unique locations around the world and ensure you have a memorable experience, eat well, sleep well and get back at serving the world better. Harmless, and I believe worth every penny, but we still fall within the "want" category and not yet a "need". For us young investors we will maintain our course to keep on building a net worth first, keep increasing our income and create other sources that would easily cover our dream trip. The worst thing that we can do is spend on our capital at this stage.

What I particularly admired is the actual city of Singapore that screams the word success on every street corner. A model of a city, probably the cleanest city in the world and absolutely no wonder why high net worth individuals value the quality of life and lifestyle available here. That city achieved a level of Excellence I am yet to see in any other and I have lived and worked in 12 countries already.

I guess it is of the utmost importance that we set for ourselves just like the city of Singapore, an impeccable level of discipline, understand the meaning of hard work, make the right choices and abide by a solid set of standards in order to achieve prosperity. It took decades for Singapore to reach such a level with an almost flawless execution. If we reverse engineer the success of this city's state, what will surface, without a doubt, are all the values to be upheld by an investor as only one path leads to propensity: Patience, Hard Work, Discipline, Resilience and Sacrifice.

Looking at the markets, it looks like they will maintain their negative trends and the good news I hope for all of you is that payday is coming in the next few days. Stock prices for some of our favorite companies are becoming quite interesting, if not a really good buy already. Choose your next steps very well, as an investment made today could be the one that will change your entire future in the next 15 years, should you stick to your decision until then.

As far as I am concerned, my eyes are kept on the Apple stock and while my other favorite companies are on an interesting discount today, I will wait for my Apple stock to reach my target price which can be very soon. A risk I am willing to take with some level of hope that the stock price will not make substantial gains until mid-July. A time they will report their Quarterly Earnings which I foresee will be impacted substantially by the US/China Trade dispute.

I did feel uneasy to be far away from the podcast for more than a day. A strange feeling as if I was not making progress and worse that I was actually letting down others that may find value or an additional support in their own journey.

Being in that city for the last few days, looking around, smelling that fresh air of success and prosperity only reinforces my will to continue right on that path. There is very little that will stop a young investor's will to double his net worth once his mind is set on winning mode.

DAY 72

As planned, once a month I will focus on what I have been able to achieve in order to grow my side business.

What is interesting is that the more I deep dive into this and into something I never thought I would be doing, the more I grow a passion for it. I have had those thoughts going through my mind on how exciting an entrepreneurial journey could be. Doing something all day long that you love deploys in you an infinite source of energy, so you easily put in the hours and giving up is certainly no longer an option.

There is no doubt in my mind that having such an opportunity in life to being able at one point to live off of doing what you are passionate about contributes to happiness in a major way. I am obviously referring to those who have been able to build such a business, as my current revenue stream from anything else than my current dividends pay outs is a perfect 0 USD.

The opportunities in 2019 to become a successful entrepreneur are infinite. Every single tool from financing, marketing and distribution can be obtained and worked out through apps right there in your hands. If that is what you aspire to do and you have not started yet, that is therefore only a question of will.

I had an objective last month to grow my followers on Instagram by 100% through the application of newly acquired skills such as creating infographics, consistently engaging with the community and putting out content daily. Well, I have failed on that objective as while I have been able to grow my followers' base by 22% only, from these 22%, probably 3% will be retained.

It is very important here to understand why I achieved such a miserable score: I will tell you. As there is no secret to success, you have to put in the work and I did not. I have not followed through on my plan. I have not walked my talk and I kept using the exact same strategy from the previous month and that did not bear fruit. As you can probably sum up from this, you are the only person that can change your future. You are the only person that is to be blamed for failure and the only person that can turn around your destiny. I did not put in the work this month and there was no progress on Instagram. I did not put a sufficient level of interest in it for me to score any sort of progress.

Another question remains, why did I lose interest and why did I not walk my talk? Why did I not match what I said I would do? I will tell you my exact feelings so that I never catch myself repeating this again or I will fail in anything I will ever start:

- I thought it would work out by itself
- I kept postponing to the next day
- I am too busy at work, this can wait
- It is too much work and too many hours a day for little immediate returns

That is the Beast I was referring to in earlier days, where there will be stretched period of times when we are vulnerable and when we are our worst enemy. It makes us human indeed one would say but would that make you a successful investor or entrepreneur or would that get you closer to your goals? Clearly not, as I have not achieved my goal this month mainly due to me, myself and I.

How do I fix this? The most powerful thing right now is to make up for this weakness, as it is a weakness until it leaves my body for good. I am accountable to myself for sure but also accountable to you and I better present some better figures next month, and I will through this mean or another.

DAY 73

This week has seen a large portion of my gains for this year wiped out. While I remain ahead with 6.5% in capital gains, such has now fallen below my 7% threshold which I aim to maintain until year end. The US/China trade war now coupled with fresh rounds of tariffs on Mexican goods and now India, spread concerns on the markets triggering sell offs of company stocks that have certain levels of dependence on China in order to do business in the US. The trade wars have touched the tech sector further as well due to the Huawei crisis and its ramifications in addition to bank stocks being hit mainly due to uncertainty in the economy following all of this. No one seems to be spared and Morgan Stanley is now putting the US economy on "recession watch".

Only one thing I can say and repeat again and again, I wish I had much more cash aside to take full advantage of this. Not enough cash as this whole crisis has happened fast, not leaving enough time to build cash from a single income but I am convinced that investment funds will jump on the opportunity in the coming weeks and generate solid profits. My second favorite stock, Bank of America has already lost close to 10% in value from the initial stock price I purchased. However, I have decided this week to focus on Apple and my next move will happen in July if all goes to plan. I will need to look at my expenses until then and yield as much cash as possible for my July move.

While the Bank of America stock is really tempting right now and it being a real chance to seriously reduce my average on it, I would prefer to increase my position in my largest investment for which I see a much larger potential for growth than a bank stock which provides, in my view, stability in my portfolio. I now need to free up some cash, work harder to create that second source of income and keep growing my dividend stocks so I can reinvest them at the end of the year for more dividend stocks.

I believe the worst thing you can do is dump your current stocks to release cash for other investments. You would probably sell them off at a loss as they stand today. However, they will recover in due time, just be patient. I would rather inject more capital, as this is the only way to continue building wealth with a prospect of serious capital growth down the line. I personally believe this could be happening. The US president is up for re-election in 2020. Every move he takes have that objective in mind and there is no better way to emerge victorious than to win or have some level of control on a trade war that he could basically curate or stop at any time, such would play quite well for him. Eventually this crisis will be over or start weakening as we get closer to the US elections to the greatest benefit of your investments made during this crisis. It will not benefit the future President to be re-elected during a full-blown recession.

DAY 74

June 3rd, 2019
Net Worth: 63,976 USD

I am first and foremost pleased to say that 51 episodes of the podcast have been published and it proves that a lot can be accomplished in two months and a half if we set our minds to it. While I am very conscious that this is very early in the process, it does validate a very important theory that we are in full control of our destiny.

It could be a podcast, a social media account you wish to grow, a business you wish to establish or a product you wish to launch. You will have very high chances that such a dream happens, and the best part of it all, we are intelligent beings capable of acquiring new skills quickly and perfect any craft provided we have the profound will to do so. We are all forces of nature; we are all capable of grand things and this day and age has opened all possible doors to enable our success. We have access to an unlimited number of learning tools, information, news, articles, books, videos and podcasts allowing us to self-educate on practically any subject we want. The internet has changed the way we learn, communicate and do business. What used to be an affair of decades to build only 15 years ago, now takes as little as months, at low cost.

I fail to understand how we still have the ability today of saying that things are impossible to accomplish or that we are stripped of all and any opportunity to have a chance at our own definition of success.

I fail to understand why or how a young man or woman today can wake up in the morning with no fire inside of them. There is not a day that passes in this world where there is not something new out there that has the potential to change your world. I have recently read that what did not exist a few years ago is now used or applied in practically everything we use. Artificial intelligence will enable the human being to be even greater in the future and being such a source of flawless expertise and assistance will only enable the human being to exceed his limits. How can we not recognize where the world is going and how we can take advantage of all of this to change our own future?

On the other hand, there are countless young people who are teaming up as we speak to create the next big thing. Young people who have taken the steps to self-educate, develop their expertise in what they love to do, open their minds to develop an idea worth pursuing, pursued that idea to transform it into a plan, developed the company, got financing despite two hundred rejects and despite countless failures, have never given up on their dreams. They have taken full advantage of what the world had to offer, regardless of their location, the level of hardship life is throwing at them, the number of kids they have to feed or the level of debt they had to clear. Most of them give everything they have in the pursuit of their dreams.

The world you currently live in has stripped you of any ability to complain or not to act. We are talking investing on the podcast and in the book, but this is just one subject of many that you have the ability to master. Life is long, and I believe that we must never stop learning, our happiness depends on it. I am 38 years old; life is still long for me. I can still try and fail countless times and still be young and stand back up again.

My objective is Financial Freedom but that is not the end game. What matters is what it will take to get there and the process of getting there is what matters to me the most. I believe that your level of success is directly proportional to the level of Sacrifice you are willing to make regardless of what your definition of success is.

We spoke at length on how to make serious adjustments to your lifestyle to build wealth. The question will remain on why you have not done so already or if you did, is this really the best you can do? Have you looked at every possible avenue already to review your current living standards not based on other people's judgement or opinions? What have you done with your salary this month that was just paid out to you? Did you go out this weekend or did you explore how you can build a better future for yourself?

Of course, this applies to all of those who are not happy with their current situation. I am not happy with my current situation, so I better walk my talk and take consistent and life changing decisions if my dream is to radically change my life as it is today. Don't feel you have arrived before even taking off.

DAY 76

As predicted, a rebound has occurred with the strongest pick up since January. While we are not back to the levels like the beginning of May, mainly due to the Chairman of the Federal Reserve of The United States signaling his openness to rate cuts amid the current trade war tensions therefore boosting stock prices.

We are invested in the long term indeed and you will say that there is therefore no use to look at our stock price daily. I will not be in agreement with that. I believe we need to stay in touch with the dynamics of the market. Stay appraised of the news impacting our investments and keep developing our understanding of how the stock market functions. As new and young investors, we are to continuously keep learning, and such cannot occur if we step away and let our investment thrive in the long term even if it will.

I would like to share today what I have been reflecting on in the past weeks, as I have a feeling that my investment strategy must continuously be re-examined as to increase my chances to reach my objectives. To recap my current strategy first:

1. Establish Yearly Budget
2. Complete review of my lifestyle and expenses to a minimum as to free up cash for the purpose of investment

3. Invest the maximum % possible of my income towards investment

4. Invest in the stock market without a third party; in companies and sectors I understand

5. Invest in Dividend paying stocks only

6. Open opportunities to create other sources of income through a side venture

I have a very strong feeling that point number 7 that I will outline here will be an important addition. However, this comes with a very high level of risk on your investment, however small, and you need to be prepared to lose it all without affecting your situation. Investing in a startup is now possible for as little as 100 USD.

Angel Investing on the other hand is still reserved to the high net worth individuals and by law you will be allowed to become an accredited investor should your household makes between 200 and 300 K USD per year or if your net worth exceeds 1.2 Million dollars I believe.

I certainly do not meet those criteria yet but there are online platforms that allow you to invest similarly but with a serious cap on your yearly investment. Such will be determined by your reported net worth excluding your home and through reporting your yearly income. As far as I am concerned, I am capped at 5000 USD per year only. However, I believe it is reasonable money to invest at high risk/high return and into startups that you will have an opportunity to look at in reasonable amount of detail. Ask questions to founders, form your own opinion and invest etc....

It is usually under the form of convertible notes. The investor would be loaning money to a startup and instead of a return in the form of principle plus interest, the investor would receive equity in the company. We would basically bet on the success of the company in the short/medium or even long term and the more successful they become, the more you receive as an investor.

I have therefore decided to create an investment fund still capped at 5000 USD per year until I increase my income and net worth to high levels. There are ways however to maximize this small yearly capital. You can invest it all into one start-up every year or break it down. I will avoid larger start-ups, focusing on very small ones asking for less capital as to maximize the investment in case the company becomes successful as your level of equity would be more substantial.

I find this line of work fascinating; the possibilities are limitless which adds fuel on my fire.

DAY 78

Let's have a look at the markets since the last days which seem to have sustained their upside momentum re-elevating gains to mid-May levels despite the trade war still ongoing. As we have all learned so far this is all subject to another bad news dropping! I am still looking forward to the opportunity to purchase more stocks should that happen and hopefully at the end of the month, so I can accumulate some more cash in the meantime. At the end of June, I will be injecting more capital from my savings in my brokerage account in the form of cash on hand and patiently wait for the next market correction.

Following the earlier days, I have been reviewing some start-ups. I have gone through the pitch of about 10 and what strikes me the most is the general level of confidence young entrepreneurs these days have on slapping a multi-million dollar valuation on an idea they have barely deployed on the market and with no sales data to back this up. While I am no Angel Investor, 5000 USD investment budget in a start-up per year is to be made with at least some form of data translating some form of performance over a period of time to base yourself on for a decision before giving away your money on a high risk.

I do realize however, that at this stage, seed investing for a young investor is dumb money as we have little expertise to bring directly into the business to make it grow to much higher valuation. It will take some more exposure as an investor to become what we call smart capital. But we are all starting in this business, so starting as such does not bother me one bit.

I hope you have scored some victories on your side this year so far, and that you are already seeing your net worth increasing month over month. I can certainly relate and I remember talking about how these little victories accumulated get you multiple steps closer to a state of constant happiness and security. Your mind expands to new limits, ideas emerge, you see light at every harbor and all of this because of you and your ability to have re-engineered your lifestyle to fit an investor mindset. How does it feel to be alive again? Do you really miss that 5 USD coffee? If you do, that is possibly a serious lack of perspective but that I will leave for another book.

I was just looking at my performance in the last 6 months and I have managed to increase my net worth by 188% through disciplined injection in capital, confident investments through research, learning above all maintaining composure in the face of mini crises. It will be much more difficult to double my current net worth, but I will certainly settle with a nice double-digit growth in the next 6 months. Do you know why I am so confident I will? Because I have a process in place that I will deviate from under no circumstances. We all have it in us, and once you start you can never stop. At the risk of repeating myself, money or the end game is not what motivates me but the process of getting there while building a new angle on life that drives me. The learning opportunities are infinite, the daily victories on self-improvement. Ultimately... Freedom... Freedom from my employer, from debt, from insecurity and from unhappiness. It can all start with a will to face your fears to invest and lower your standards of living. Free yourself from other people's opinions and slowly take off.

Money does not equal to Happiness, but you can be sure it fixes 90% of your problems which is not so bad of a step towards happiness... After that, the remaining 10% are in your hands.

DAY 79

June 8th, 2019
Net Worth: 68,233.65 USD

Let's first outline what was successful about the last week. Well we have made our gains back to May levels and let me tell you, by not giving ourselves away to our emotions and by not ceding to panic and doing something stupid like selling off your stocks at the first sign of a drop. I have recovered 105% of my gains within the week, by simply not reacting, the same would have happened if I had closed my eyes for a full week. I have not sold a single stock since the beginning of the year, my net worth increased by more than 188% at yesterday's close despite everything that happened since. I am no investment guru. While these gurus beat us all even by 10X, we work with humility, we are just starting and every point we gain are a tremendous victory. So well done to you and your sensational ability to have set yourself up for success.

The week ahead for me will be marked by a business trip to Bangkok as I still have a job and as we have said before, in order to keep increasing your income you must excel in your current profession until freedom is possible. It must be a job that you love or this will never work. I manage two luxury resorts in a remote location in Asia, remote enough to call my current lifestyle a full blown sacrifice for my wife and I. However, we are fully aware of Why we do this and it makes it all easier, on top of loving what I do. To add a little bit more color, I was entrusted to oversee six months of construction, pre-opening and opening activities for one of the resorts which successfully opened seven months ago and finally manage a cluster of two hotels. So, this week will be about me presenting our Quarterly performance, line by line to our Billionaire Chairman & Founder, our CEO and the C-Suite of our listed hospitality company.

This is a quarterly exercise which is always stressful but less when you ensure you run the business. Never give up as your main source of income must be protected at all costs if you wish to keep on investing. To be perfectly honest, it is always good to see and take notes from our Chairman, a self-made billionaire whose vision exceeds yours by being able to see 20 years down the line. There are different breeds of people in the world and we can only but be inspired by them.

So much so that we begin building aspirations to achieve as much as they did by applying probably the exact same principles for success that you can read, listen or view everywhere else. The difference between them and us is that they are decades into the game, so you can't compare your own current success or envy theirs, as we are just at chapter one.

This week will therefore be for me to survive the Corporate environment as I am usually a pro-operator and less of a board person. I believe in what is being done in the trenches with my teams rather than anything else, so again this will be far out of my comfort zone which is the only way to keep on progressing. I believe you should only evolve where the air is rarified, it is just more fun than staying put.

It is just like re-evaluating your lifestyle your expenses, your savings, starting investing from zero. Only radical changes bring about radical progress. So this week, just like me, evolve outside your comfort zone, do or start a project that you would have never thought you could possibly do. When was the last time you met a hotelier who is the host of a podcast on investing?

DAY 80

I hope you are fully geared for the week and that you have already placed your right foot outside your comfort zone and made the decision to start something new that have an aim to get you closer to your objectives. A few good news dropped in the past few days as far as my work and the podcast are concerned. One of my properties just received a very valuable international recognition of Excellence. I got the chance to be asked to write an article on Entrepreneurship for my company, and I did, I submitted it today. The podcast has entered the top charts in the US and in the UK, well still a few pages down the charts but I consider this a tremendous victory.

What have I learned here, is that if you execute with resilience and passion in anything you set your mind on doing, you will get some form of return and I am not talking money; as it is not the primary objective. The return is an additional stone on your path towards your continued self-development. One stone after the other will ultimately lead to Financial Freedom. There are no shortcuts, no hacks, the path is built one stone at a time and it is not a straight one either, but how gratifying it is to lay that next stone onto it! I have a feeling your next stone will be laid this week because you would have taken a major decision.

I will be honest with you however, it has been a while now that I have been feeling that my sacrifice being in this location was too great. After travelling a little, I kept on wishing I was somewhere else to pursue my plan. Since 65% of the podcast listeners are from the United States, I will say that I thought of them and what they could be accomplishing as there is no better place on Earth where you can achieve your greatest aspirations. You must believe that, as I have seen enough of the world to tell you that if your mind is set on the right mode as of today, there is practically nothing you can't achieve, only by being right where you are at this very minute and by investing in yourself.

As an Investor, the most profitable investment you can make is in yourself. Being an Investor is not just saving and investing. I believe it is a philosophy, an angle taken on your life that sets you up for success in anything you decide to pursue. Ask yourself probably, what was your latest investment in yourself? I have not invested enough in myself and I am starting to feel the effects which led me drifting towards giving up even if it is for a second, and it does show that I still have that feeling of entitlement that I must shake off. How can I ever complain? We are way too fortunate to complain and I will let you list out the reasons why I would say something like that whatever your situation is. Be honest with yourself on this one. Now that is cleared out of the way, let's keep going, shall we?

DAY 84

It took me a whole day to reach Bangkok again from home. The most inefficient way of travelling remains airports and planes, and for that I have tremendous respect for Elon Musk and his vision to disrupt the way we travel. I would hop on his Hyperloop any day as I hate to fly. I have completed my Quarterly review for my company. It was a hard one this year, picture yourself in a conference room with 80 people, a panel of high level executives, yourself sitting in front of your billionaire Chairman & Founder, your CEO and the C Suite of your company, two hotels to present, 60 slides and a microphone. This is a highly uncomfortable position; it is hard and unless you are 55 years old, with 35 years of experience doing this there is no way you'll be comfortable in there. This was me protecting my only real source of income. Now I would like you to picture the exact same situation, the exact same set up, however you have managed to build two other sources of income excluding your investments. I am certain I would have approached these quarterly reviews or any hard situation for that matter differently, as I would already know that the stakes would not be as high, that I am safe, that I have a choice. That is what Financial Freedom brings along as well. I am also certain that such a peace of mind would allow you to excel even more at your current profession. Currently my second revenue stream from my dividends is 93 USD/month on average. I am not even close.

Let's talk investing. After observing the stock markets movement for the last two years on daily basis and given the roller coaster we are currently in, I am now able to confidently confirm to you that unless a major crisis hits us, there is absolutely no reason to fear any correction in the markets. I am not saying you should fear a major crisis but I believe you should be prepared for one, at least I will. These market corrections will occur every year once or twice and just to be precise, a market correction is when a market drops from 10 to 19%. A drop of 20% or more or a bear market will occur usually every 5 years and we have been running already without one for a decade but in any case and historically speaking, a bull market always follows a bear market. So it simply comes down again to Patience. Something most of us lack of as we want everything to happen right away, it is just in our nature. In other words, rather than spending your time fearing a downturn, you should use the same level of energy to build a real infrastructure around yourself that will allow you to consistently save, invest and build wealth.

I did think about this yesterday and I believe it is extremely important: I am not sharing my name on the podcast until the book comes out. I am calling myself "The Young Investor", as this is who I am, a beginner and early in the process just like you.

If I had to make a podcast on hospitality or hotel management, I would have certainly already earned the right to put my name out there as there are measurable achievements for more than a decade. If you do look at the podcast and the book details on each episode and headlines you will see that I share the value of my holdings as it grows and so far, I have only reached my first milestone. However, the idea of this all is to prove overtime that it is possible for anyone who had a history similar to mine being a full blown consumer who had no love for his future self, to re-engineer himself and mindset, radically change his lifestyle, adjust his spending, invest and be on his way to build wealth.

This is real, these initiatives and the sacrifices that you are willing to take will simply change your life. I am still learning, still changing my approach, still asking myself plenty of questions on how to do better. I am still curious about everything, still experimenting. One day I will earn the right to put my name out there and anyone could use this experience and achievements so that any young investor can go back to all podcast episodes, the book and follow the same path. Anyone can learn as much from success than from failure, let's see where this journey leads me.

I came across this statistic recently. On average, only 8% of the 25-34-year-old are investing their earnings, this is low, very low. I can't begin to imagine the reasons behind this, but you are not part of these stats.

DAY 86

There is always one thing that looms over your head whenever you are at that stage of making up your mind, whether it is to jump into your investing journey or keep going well into it, that would be when will that next Financial Crisis occur? Will I lose all my hard earned money? The time and effort I have put into structuring my financial future? It used to be the excuse I told myself at the time I believed that it was better to spend it all, rather than to potentially lose it all on the stock market. At least I would get the goods.

Now that I am well into my journey, I will share with you how I approach that exact same situation today and how I personally will approach the next crisis which will inevitably happen. Historically speaking, a Financial Crisis and recession in the US economy occurs every 5 years and we have been running without one for the last 10 years, so I would say it is about time; I presume. A couple of things are important to remember as a young investor. First and foremost is that the US economy and its stock market have always emerged stronger from a serious financial crisis since the beginning of its history. Even through World Wars, which I believe are the worst possible events affecting world economies, we are now doing better than ever.

Therefore, we probably will need to revert back to the earliest one in 2008, where we will use the S&P 500 as an indicator which actually represents the market capitalization of the 500 largest companies in the United States. It is just *the* reference index telling you the actual temperature of the US stock exchange and the economy. For those of you who were old enough to have lived through it, you will remember that it was a pretty bad situation. Your investments would have lost about 35% of their value on average if not more. The crash of September 2008 lasted until July 2009, less than a year and then returned 26.4% that year. The markets fully recovered, and we know the story since then. We can even go back to the previous bear market in 2000/2001/2002, which also recovered the following year. Slightly more extended but still with a full and stronger recovery.

I will understand if you feel that injecting money during these periods would be a serious risk, but I think there is every reason to trust the US economy for the next 100 years. It will always recover and recover stronger. It is a question of trust and patience. During those times, and in the event that no extreme situation occurs in my life as a result of it, such as losing my job and my sources of income, I will be keeping my positions and using all my cash on hand to buy more stocks and simply continue on with my investment strategy regardless.

You can then buy great companies for pennies on the dollar which will give you never before seen returns once the markets are fully recovered and start generating serious returns. I do know that such could take three years but do not be in a hurry to see returns. Rather be grateful that the markets are giving us 2 to 3 years to do our shopping! Just stay the course, and simply make peace with the fact that your current investments now will lose 30 to 50% of their value at one point in time. It is inevitable and if one already knows that this is going to happen, then you have enough time to prepare mentally, financially and evaluate the risk you are willing to take as of today.

Do you know the difference between the majority of the audience and readers and the rest of the world? It is that you are between 18 and 35 years old, so we are in possession of the strongest and most valuable commodity..... we have TIME and a lot of it. Please research the history of returns of the Dow Jones and the S&P 500, see for yourself and answer that question for me: How much return the S&P500 would have given you today if you were fortunate enough to have made an investment in 2008?

I rest my case...

I now know without a doubt in my mind, my strategy through what can be characterized as the best possible case scenario for an investor and the worst-case scenario for a day trader.

I am about to go on another business trip…5 hours' drive through the rice paddy fields!

DAY 87

My hopes of acquiring more Apple shares at Q4 2018 price are slowly fading away as it does seem another dialogue between China and the US is going to happen soon, bringing again the hopes up for a resolution of the trade war. As you could probably note, the S&P 500 closed more than 1% up following this news.

Headline investing is a completely different approach, unpredictable, minute by minute and very high risk... not for us young investors. At this stage of our investing journey, I feel it is better to stay structured and methodical as the most difficult phase, I believe, is building the foundations that will allow us to continuously and systematically build wealth in the long term. In my earlier days as an expert consumer, I had a very different understanding of what building wealth required. I was convinced that it was not for me, but only reserved to a select few, reserved to the high net worth individuals.

What I failed to understand is that a large portion of the select few did start exactly as I did. However they developed a level of financial maturity and self-awareness at a much earlier stage. Creating wealth is as simple as spending less than you earn and investing those savings into stocks or other forms of instruments that you value and understand at the right time and at the right price.

To make it easier, if you are looking at 10-15 years down the line, the right time is now, and the right price is now as the stock market and ultimately your investments will look a lot different in a decade or more and usually way up. I will certainly not be able to value a company with an accuracy level down to the penny and my investments are not substantial enough for a penny more or less to matter than much in my opinion. So if I am off by a dollar or two, that's really not a big deal for me and even the most astute investors have at times overpaid for stocks. However, they still did very well just not as well as they could have. So what? I am not motivated by greed but rather by continuous improvement in whatever forms.

Everything is improving so far, personally, financially, professionally and emotionally. I have no doubt in my mind that this is all happening because I have created a purpose for myself. All of this compounded the day I have started my investing journey and flipped my lifestyle into one that makes absolute sense for me and which now supports a bright future.

I had a look at the podcast stats this morning, how interesting to see that young investors are growing and that the subject of investing is of high interest. To all young investors, this is probably the best time in history to become an investor as the access to the stock market and the ability to make investments were made easy for all, only when the internet hit the scale we know today. Financial literacy will be hitting larger portion of populations around the world, the number of investors will substantially grow and at a very rapid pace. The investment you will make today are pennies compared to what a stock may cost to acquire once the number of investors around the world hits an all-time high.

People do not spend as they use to. People are becoming conscious about their money and about the value of money. It is time that you do as well and on your own, do not entrust your money with a third party, learn the craft.

DAY 91

All my lost gains have now been recovered; the Federal Reserve of the United States have maintained their interest rates. Such is most probably due to the fact that the trade war between the US and China has actually created more economic activity within the United States. The economy is healthy and strong. There is no need to boost it further at this stage while putting them down is still considered. Investors' confidence is temporarily back once again, markets closed on a positive note. These are the quick deadlines.

Only 9 days to go until the end of the month and I have no doubt that you have managed to score some great savings this month as I did. As I told you in the beginning of the month, I had set an objective to ensure I have built up enough cash to increase my position in Apple stocks. The stock recovered strong and that may no longer be possible for now. I am looking forward to see how this impacted their quarterly earnings but I doubt I will have the opportunity to buy at my price target which is close to 50 USD below the current price. It could have been possible should the recent headline had escalated. Apple is expected to release their next Quarterly Earnings on July 30th. There is still more time and I wanted to share my reasoning on how I am approaching this whole situation:

1. I set my sight on a company I wish to purchase; in this case I aimed at increasing my current positions in Apple.

2. The Apple investment I made last year paid off and gained 38.5% so far. It will certainly be difficult to get back to last year stock price level. Should I make a substantial investment today, my average would increase substantially. There are two things here to consider:

   a. What would be the acceptable average/stock price Apple is worth for me to increase my position at a higher price today?

   b. Set that new price as a target and initiate the process to make my investment.

3. I started building cash since my last investment with that objective in mind which will be cumulated with past savings, current savings and the July income.

4. Wait for the earnings to be released which I anticipate would hit negatively. The stock price given China represents 20% of Apple Top Line revenues and the lasted news about Apple who are studying relocating 15 to 30% of their production outside of China is a hint into what the next earning call will sound like.

I will be ready with some serious buying power from now until the end of July. However, I will also consider the risk that everything may return to a certain degree of normality between the US and China until then. Two reasons for this: The G20 will happen on the 28th and 29th of June. President Trump and President Xi Jinping of China will meet and hold talks. Things could evolve positively hence affecting how Apple stock price up, no one knows.

I am not going into any more technicalities. It is my own judgement and strategy and I do not base it on hundreds of hours of TV or listening to financial analysts. I am certain you can come up with similar reasoning on any other stock provided you are genuinely interested in the companies you own or wish to own, stay appraised, do your research. Don't complicate things there, I think the key here is not the headlines but your ability to sacrifice and save to build that buying power allowing you to be an investor.

Do not lose sights of our purpose. Our aim is Freedom and that comes with Sacrifice and you must be willing to understand what that means in this context.

DAY 94

In earlier days, I remember saying that I wish I had the opportunity growing up or while being in my 20's to have been able to refer myself to a podcast, a book or a comprehensive website that could guide me on the first steps to take towards starting my investment journey. The problem was that the internet had not yet hit scale and I guess I may have been too lazy to pick up books or go and sit with my banker or do anything with regards to my financial future for that matter in order to educate myself better and open a brokerage account.

I have solid news; we are in 2019 and every possible tool is available at your fingertip in order to start the journey. It seems like every possible excuse not to, have simply been eliminated from one day to the next. Since starting my journey, I have used series of apps and sites to set myself up with tools I regularly use for my personal finance, budgeting, investing, financial/tailor made news and for my side ventures to create other streams of income. With all that is available for one to start, I have been able in less than 2 years to:

- Self-Educate about Investing and Corporate Finance
- Open a brokerage account and start my first investment
- Stay laser focused on the news relevant to my investments
- Budget my expenses for the whole year and track those expenses down to the cent

- Start a podcast and distribute it on all platforms
- Set up a website and design it
- Write and distribute a book

That is amongst other things that I am working on at skeleton stage right now but I may not have been in a position to do so without the existence of the internet and all these developers around the world making our lives easier day by day. The internet has liberated the world and I am now able to work with experts from every continent online and with exceptional skills, if I so wish, to assist me in translating any strategy into actual results.

I do not have to go through a third party for this. No boardroom, and no endless administration, only a platform that allows all these professionals to connect with me and do business in a matter of a few clicks. With that in mind, there is nothing that can't be achieved if your heart follows your passion to make it work; subsequently, your legs to get out of that couch.

I was looking through my brokerage firm platform today, not only is it now very easy to invest, there is an endless source of information there for the investor. All the data is available from your bed, to ensure you have enough information to make your investments: News, Research, Market analysis, historical data and in-depth data. It is just there for us, while getting access to such information pre-internet age was for the select few.

We all have a shot at building serious wealth Ladies and Gentlemen. The only obstacle for this ever to happen resides within you as it lived within me before opening my eyes to the possibilities the world offers us today and what I had missed. I have no regrets, as I am doubling down today to catch up.

I mean, it was as easy as me thinking this morning at 6.00am how I am looking at allocating 15% of my capital towards Real Estate Investment. I will certainly not do this without studying the sector and determining if I am passionate enough to invest in it. I am not a real estate person, but I will be in a matter of weeks, thanks to the wealth of information available to me. It was at 6.00am, that I picked up my phone and simply Googled the basics and I knew more about real estate at 7.00am than I ever did. Obviously at amateur level but better educated already, and guess what, I am interested in knowing more, that is a very good sign.

DAY 96

Markets ended on the negative and my holdings were down by 1.25%. There are at the moment quite a bit happening in the world that have the potential to impact your investments. I will always stand by my strong convictions that I must, stay invested, be patient and play the long-term game. These headlines will disappear to give way to others. Our investments will keep growing with ups and downs for sure along the journey. At macro level, they will be way up, I have faith in the US economy. Literally, just now, the US secretary of Treasury announced that the trade deal with China progressed and pre-market indicates a strong opening in a few hours.

It is interesting to summarize a little, the major headlines and each subject to other headlines that could make your stock soar or plunge in seconds.

- Trade war and tariffs between US and China, the largest economies in the word. Businesses are cancelling investments in Asia as a result.

- Serious tensions with Iran

- Tension with North Korea

- Tensions with Russia

- New Prime Minister in the UK coupled with the Brexit

All of these have the potential to start a chain of events that could lead the world economy into chaos, but they don't. The ability of such headlines to keep the world composed and controlled despite their power to destroy is very interesting to me. As if everyone is agreeing to disagree.

So far, and despite all of this, the ups and downs, the drama in the news; my holdings are ahead by 13.5% this year. It does seem that the house always wins, that the stock market is stronger than any of this. Even at times of the worst crisis the world has ever known, it does seem it recovers better and stronger. This is will not change, us human beings keep evolving. Our economies and our societies evolve with us. This is the greatest period in human history to be alive, as we get to see the transition from one age to the other. One more reason for you to start your journey today or this will be the most important train you'll ever miss.

On another note, on my side venture front, some progress was made. I was interested in knowing more about Affiliate Marketing, which is basically generating revenue through affiliate programs driven by companies in every sector by using a link specifically generated for you that you place on your website. Should website visitors be interested in that product, they will click that link, make the purchase and you would get a commission. I was excited about it I must admit; the whole idea had some substance to cover the costs of the podcast and the book at least. I went along with it for a few days, got approved on many programs, built an additional section on my website with companies young and new investors could start their journey with, good companies, relevant for us for sure.

However, I quickly changed my mind and I took everything down yesterday after only 48 hours, deleted all the accounts and took the new section down from my website. It did not feel right to become an affiliate marketer and support a system to monetize my website or anything at this stage. I am way too early in the process to ask for anything and when you want it too fast, you generally crash. I believe the most important thing right now is to share my journey with the highest number of young and new investors, stay in touch with the community and hope we can contribute to the success of one another.

I do deviate from time to time, this is in my nature, but I now quickly manage a turnaround with these type of thoughts. Quick gains, impatience and lack of discipline all form the enemy inside of you and me. I almost lost a few days ago, but you can be sure I will not fall in that trap again.

As a matter of transparency, all the activities I am doing currently on the podcast and Instagram or other platforms, the experts I consult or hire, these activities are solely aimed at connecting with other young and new investors as to make this podcast and the book available to whoever it can support. I wished I had one I could listen to and wake up earlier to investing. I will aim at staying informative about the subject while going through the same journey with you.

DAY 97

June 27th, 2019
Net Worth: 74,899.28 USD

Mr. Warren Buffett, the legendary investor, has said something that stuck with me, "Nobody buys a farm based on whether they think it is going to rain next year, they buy it because they think it is a good investment over 10 or 20 years". That right there summarizes the investment strategy and mindset to adopt. Buying stocks is buying a piece of a company and the only approach that would make any sense, is to buy a company that unless the world economy melts away in the next 5 years will still be around in the next 10 years and after that let the market do its job and build wealth for you.

I have been looking at Real Estate Investment Trusts or REIT, which allows individual investors to buy shares in commercial real estate portfolio that receive income from a variety of properties. As I did mention, I was looking at investing about 15% of my capital in real estate and REIT are a way to do it via your brokerage account which will allow you to avoid all the hassle that can come from owning actual brick and mortar. It is certainly cheaper and it pays solid dividends as well.

What remains for me to do is to extract the best REIT out there, dig into their numbers, ask fellow investors their opinions, read on them and try and come up with my own investment decision and it may not happen at all as well. We need to remember that we are in the "Buy and Hold" investment strategy and you need to be able to confidently buy a stock out of utmost trust and confidence that it will create wealth for you in the long term. You may feel that what I just said lacks practicality, how are you in fact going to recognize the best company you should invest in? You are not Warren Buffett, they call him the Oracle of Omaha as if he could predict how a stock can perform 10 years down the line. He certainly cannot but he did put in the work to identify them. His investments are public, and you can start by looking at those to determine which company at least is worth looking into.

The price he purchased them for are usually unknown but through your research you could easily have an idea or a range at least, giving you a sense of how early he took position. What is the stock price he increased his position at? If he did through a certain time period. At what point of time in the history of the company in question he increased or decreased his position? Extract his average price positioning for that company, there are plenty of ways to do research for your investment. Luckily, we have access today to every information we desire, he did not and that is why he can be qualified as an investing genius.

Warren Buffett is a good start. A personality in the investment community who the young and new investors can start reading about, listening to and certainly get into his mind as the gentleman is an absolute reference. You will find that throughout his articles, his letters to his own shareholders as Chairman of Berkshire Hathaway and interviews, that he keeps on saying the same principles of investing.

"Buy wonderful companies and hold the stock for 10 to 20 years and you will do well."

As far as he is concerned, he is not looking at selling some of his stocks at all and in perpetuity. That is how his company will flourish as it already did, today making him the third wealthiest man on the planet.

He has certainly influenced me to start investing and I hold stocks which he can easily consider as wonderful companies.

DAY 100

The G20 did have its effects on the markets, a most positive one. On earlier days, I did mention that we can undoubtedly expect the relations between US and China to ease up a little and the talks towards a trade agreement to resume. Now this is all temporary of course as the truce will not fix the problems. Another headline will affect this very soon, just expect it and factor this in. We will get back to this later. President Trump stepped into North Korea, which shows how tensions can be managed generally through diplomacy rather than force. Diplomacy is good for the markets and this is where we stand at the moment and this buys us a little more time.

Allow me to clarify. In the last few days we have seen the markets recovering and even the S&P 500 again reached an all-time high on Monday and the Dow Jones Industrial average as well. These indexes tell you the temperature on the markets, quite good following the G20. If you deep dive a little into your research, other indicators are showing negative signs pointing towards a possible recession.

Let's keep this simple, all of this does not matter to me at all. There will be highs, there will be lows throughout our journey. I will step back when the markets are good and step in full force when the markets are in turmoil. Again, it does not matter... it is all a win/win situation anyway.

What I have also learned since, is that once you have established your own financial structure and system around yourself that supports you towards freeing capital for investment, and I mean here regardless of the amount or what you are able to commit, as the important thing is to save. Once this is established, the routine of creating wealth will establish itself as well.

Here is the little formula I find to be the simplest I could put into words to build wealth:

Right now the markets are strong, healthy and doing well = the stocks are expensive = I keep my saved cash until the markets start to correct or in crisis again as they always do = I buy stocks again of dividend paying companies I understand and love at the price I have determined to be appropriate through my research = I make a buy and hold it for 10 to 15 years

What I look at currently is that my gains so far this year, stand at 19%. The only thing that could happen that would wipe out all my gains and allow me to buy more stocks is an actual Financial Crisis happening this year, 19% loss is substantial. I am still waiting for the Apple earnings call end of July, but I doubt that I will have a major buy opportunity given the recent news highly favorable to Apple.

Since Day 1, my Net Worth grew by 55%.

Today is the start of your next 100 days...

www.ingramcontent.com/pod-product-compliance
Lightning Source LLC
Chambersburg PA
CBHW021419210526
45463CB00001B/450